Data Communications
Pocket Book

Other Pocket Books from Heinemann Newnes

Data Communications Pocket Book

Second Edition

Michael Tooley

Butterworth-Heinemann Ltd
Linacre House, Jordan Hill, Oxford OX2 8DP

 PART OF REED INTERNATIONAL BOOKS

OXFORD   LONDON   BOSTON
MUNICH   NEW DELHI   SINGAPORE   SYDNEY
TOKYO   TORONTO   WELLINGTON

First published 1989
Reprinted 1990
Second edition 1992

British Library Cataloguing in Publication Data
Tooley, Michael H.
Data Communications pocket book. – 2nd ed.
– (Pocket books)
1. Microcomputer systems. Data transmission.
I. Title
004.6

ISBN 0 7506 0427 1

Printed and bound in Great Britain

Preface

Few can doubt that we are witnessing a revolution in communications of a scale unsurpassed since the invention of the printing press. An important facet of this information revolution is that new technology has provided us with the key to a hitherto unimaginable wealth of knowledge – a virtually limitless fund of information covering multitudinous facets of human endeavour. This vast resource is commonly available almost anywhere in the world and we now have virtually instantaneous access to any part of it.

An essential pre-requisite to accessing this fund of information is the establishment of data communications systems which allow information to be quickly and easily exchanged between computers and other intelligent processing devices. This new sphere of activity has been instrumental in providing an added dimension to the use of computer systems; not only does it provide a means of exchanging information between computers at remote sites but it also permits efficient sharing of resources within local area networks (LANs).

This book presents, in as succinct a manner as possible, information of everyday relevance to the world of data communications. Despite the apparent complexity of the subject, care has been taken to ensure that the book is meaningful to those with little, or no, technical expertise. To this end, tabulated reference material has been interspersed with brief explanatory text and relevant diagrams. As an example, the section dealing with local area networks contains introductory paragraphs which explain what a LAN is and what it does before continuing to describe the important features of several of the most popular networking standards. Readers already familiar with the principles of networking will be able to ignore the introductory paragraphs and refer directly to the system specific information. The newcomer, however, will be rather more concerned with general concepts and should thus benefit from a study of the introductory material.

The book should be invaluable to anyone involved with the interconnection of computer systems: technicians and engineers involved with the installation, commissioning and maintenance of data communications equipment, executives and clerical staff (who are end users of data communications related products), and managers involved with the specification and purchasing of data communications related products and systems. The book should also appeal to the ever-increasing band of enthusiasts wishing to exploit data communications in connection with home management and leisure pursuits.

Finally, readers should be aware that this book has not been designed with readability in mind. Rather, it has been arranged so that information can be accessed quickly and easily. The book is intended to form an integral part of the reader's everyday 'toolkit', not merely left on the shelf for occasional reading!

Michael Tooley

Contents

Abbreviations commonly used in data communications

AAT	arbitrated access timer
ABM	asynchronous balanced mode
AC	alternating current
AC	access control
ACD	automatic call distributor
ACIA	asynchronous communications interface adapter
ACK	acknowledge
ACU	auto-call unit
ADCCP	advanced data communication control procedure
ADLC	add-on data link control
ADPCM	adaptive pulse code modulation
AF	audio frequency
ALOHA	(an experimental radio broadcast network)
AM	amplitude modulation
ARM	asynchronous response mode
ARQ	automatic request for repetition
ASCII	American standard code for information interchange
ASK	amplitude-shift keying
ASR	automatic send/receive
ATDM	asynchronous time division multiplexing
BCC	block check character
BCD	binary coded decimal

BCS	binary synchronous communications
BDLC	Burroughs data link control
BIOS	basic input/output system
bps	bits per second
CANTAT	Canada transatlantic telephony cable
CASE	common applications service elements
CATV	community antenna television (ie, cable TV)
CBX	computerized branch exchange
CCP	communications control program
CCS	common-channel signalling
CCU	communications control unit
CD	carrier detect
CFR	Cambridge fast ring
CHI	communications hardware interface
CILE	call information logging equipment
CODEC	coder-decoder
CPU	central processing unit
CRA	call routing apparatus
CRC	cyclic redundancy check
CRT	cathode ray tube
CSMA	carrier sense multiple access
CSMA/CA	CSMA with collision avoidance
CSMA/DA	CSMA with collision detection
CSPCN	circuit-switched public data network
CTA	circuit terminating equipment
CTS	clear to send
CUG	closed user group
CVSD	continuously variable slope delta modulation
DA	destination address
DAA	data access arrangement
DART	dual asynchronous receiver/transmitter
DASS	digital access signalling system
dB	decibel
DC	direct current
DCE	data circuit-terminating equipment
DDCMP	digital data communication message protocol
DDI	direct dial-in
DDS	digital data service
DDS	Dataphone digital services
DDN	digital data network
DES	data encryption standard
DNIC	data network identification code
DPNSS	digital private network signalling system
DPSK	differential phase-shift keying
DSB	double sideband
DSC	district switching centre
DTE	data terminal equipment
EBCDIC	extended binary coded decimal interchange code
EBX	electronic branch exchange
ED	ending delimiter
EDU	error detecting unit
EFT	electronic funds transfer
ELR	earthed loop
ENQ	enquiry
EOT	end of transmission
EPoS	electronic point of sale
EPSS	experimental packet switching service
ETB	end of transmitted block
ETX	end of text

FAX	facsimile
FC	frame control
FCS	frame check sequence
FDM	frequency division multiplexing
FEC	forward error control
FM	frequency modulation
FS	frame status
FSK	frequency-shift keying
FTAM	file transfer applications and management
FTP	file transfer protocol
GSC	group switching centre
HDB3	high-density bipolar code no. 3
HDLC	high-level data link control
HF	high frequency
HM	hybrid modulation
HSLN	high-speed local network
Hz	Hertz
IA5	international alphabet no. 5
ICP	interconnection protocol
IDA	integrated digital access
IDD	international direct dialling
IDN	integrated digital network
ILD	injector laser diode
IMP	interface message processor
INFO	information
I/O	input/output
IPMS	interpersonal message processor
IPSS	international packet-switched service
ISD	international subscriber dialling
ISDN	integrated services digital network
ISPBX	integrated services private automatic branch exchange
ITA2	international telegraph alphabet no. 2
JTMP	joint transfer and manipulation protocol
kHz	kilohertz
KTS	key telephone system
LAM	line adapter module
LAN	local area network
LAP	link access protocol
LAPB	link access protocol balanced
LCD	liquid crystal display
LED	light emitting diode
LD	loop disconnect
LLC	logical link control
LF	low frequency
LRC	longitudinal redundancy check
LSB	lower sideband
LSI	large scale integration
LT	line termination
LTE	line terminating equipment
LWT	listen while talk
MAC	medium access control
MAP	manufacturing automation protocol
MAU	multi-station access unit
MCVF	multi-channel voice frequency
MF	multiple frequency
MF	medium frequency
MHS	message handling system
MHz	megahertz

MPX	multiplexer
MSC	main switching centre
MTA	message transfer agent
MTBF	mean time between failure
MTTR	mean time to repair
MTTF	mean time to failure
NAK	negative acknowledgement
NCC	network control centre
NCOP	network code of practice
NIFTP	network-independent file transfer protocol
NITS	network-independent transport service
NMU	network management unit
NOC	network operations centre
NORE	nominal overall reference equivalent
NRM	normal response mode
NRZ	non-return to zero
NT	network termination
NT1	network terminal no. 1
NTE	network terminating equipment
NTU	network terminating unit
NUA	network user address
OSI	open systems interconnection
PABX	private automatic branch exchange
PAD	packet assembler/disassembler
PAM	pulse amplitude modulation
PAT	priority access timer
PAX	private automatic exchange
PBX	private branch exchange
PC	personal computer
PCI	pre-connection inspection
PCM	pulse code modulation
PDN	public data network
P/F	poll/final
PM	phase modulation
PM	pulse modulation
PMBX	private manual branch exchange
PMR	private mobile radio
POS	point of sale
PPM	pulse position modulation
pps	pulses per second
PSDN	packet switched data network
PSE	packet switching exchange
PSK	phase-shift keying
PSPDN	packet-switched public data network
PSS	packet switched service
PSS	Packet SwitchStream
PSTN	public switched telephone network
PTO	public telecommunications operator
PTT	post, telegraph and telephone
PVC	permanent virtual circuit
PWM	pulse width modulation
QAM	quadrature amplitude modulation
QPSK	quadrature phase-shift keying
QSAM	quadrature sideband amplitude modulation
RBT	remote batch terminal
RF	radio frequency
RFS	ready for sending
RJE	remote job entry
ROM	read-only memory

RT	resynchronization timer
RTS	request to send
RZ	return to zero
SA	source address
SAP	service access point
SCRA	single-line call-routing apparatus
SCVF	single-channel voice frequency
SD	starting delimiter
SDLC	synchronous data link control
SIO	serial input/output
SMTA	single-line multi-extension telephone apparatus
SNA	systems network architecture
SNDCF	subnetwork-dependent convergence facility
SNICF	subnetwork-independent convergence facility
SNR	signal-to-noise ratio
SOH	start of heading
SPC	stored program control
SSB	single sideband
SSB-SC	single sideband suppressed carrier
STD	subscriber trunk dialling
STDM	statistical time division multiplexer
STS	space-time-space
STX	start of text
SVC	switched virtual circuit
SYN	synchronous idle
TA	terminal adapter
TAN	trunk access node
TBR	timed break
TCM	trellis code modulation
TCP	transmission control protocol
TDM	time division multiplexing
TDMA	time division multiple access
TE	terminal equipment
TIP	terminal interface processor
TJF	test jack frame
TOP	technical and office protocol
TSE	terminal-switched exchange
TST	time-space-time
TXE	electronic exchange
TXK	crossbar exchange
UA	user access
UART	universal asynchronous receiver/transmitter
UHF	ultra high frequency
USART	universal synchronous/asynchronous receiver/ transmitter
USB	upper sideband
VADS	value-added data service
VAN	value added network
VANS	value-added network service
VDU	visual display unit
VHF	very high frequency
VRC	vertical redundancy check
VSB	vestigial sideband
VTP	virtual terminal protocol
WAN	wide area network
WF	wait flag

Abbreviations used for advisory bodies and other organisations

ACTs	advisory committees on telecommunications
ANSI	American National Standards Institute
ARPA	Advanced Research Projects Agency
ASA	American Standards Association
AT&T	American Telephone and Telegraph Corporation
BABT	British Approvals Board for Telecommunications
BEITA	Business Equipment and Information Technology Trade Association
BFIC	British Facsimile Industry Consultative Committee
BREEMA	British Radio and Electronic Equipment Manufacturers' Association
BSI	British Standards Institution
BT	British Telecom
CCITT	International Telephone and Telegraph Consultative Committee
CEPT	European Conference of Postal and Telecommunications Administrations
COMSAT	Communications Satellite Corporation
DTI	Department of Trade and Industry
EARN	European Academic Research Network
ECMA	European Computer Manufacturer's Association
EEA	Electronic Engineering Association
EIA	Electronics Industries Association
FCC	Federal Communications Commission
IBM	International Business Machines
IEE	Institution of Electrical Engineers
IEEE	Institution of Electrical and Electronic Engineers
IEEIE	Institution of Electrical and Electronics Incorporated Engineers
IERE	Institution of Electronic and Radio Engineers
INTELSAT	International Telecommunications Satellite Consortium
ISO	International Standards Organisation
ITU	International Telecommunication Union
NBS	National Bureau of Standards
NCC	National Computing Centre
PATACS	Posts and Telecommunications Advisory Committee
PTT	Postal, Telegraph and Telephone authority
SITA	Société Internationale de Telecommunication Aeronautique
SWIFT	Society for Worldwide Interbank Financial Telecommunications
TEMA	Telecommunication Engineering and Manufacturing Association
TMA	Telecommunications Managers Association

Manufacturers' prefixes for semiconductor devices

AD	Analog Devices
AD	Intersil

AH	National Semiconductor
AM	AMD
AY	General Instrument
C	Intel
CD, CDP	RCA
CP	General Instrument
D	Intel
DG	Siliconix
DM	National Semiconductor
DMPAL	National Semiconductor
DS	National Semiconductor
DS	Signetics
DS	Texas Instruments
DP	AMD
DP	National Semiconductor
EF	Thomson/EFCIS
F	Fairchild
F	Ferranti
G	GTE
H	SGS
HCMP	Hughes
HD	Hitachi
HEF	Mullard
HEF	Signetics
HM	Hitachi
HN	Hitachi
I	Intel
ICL	Intersil
ICM	Intersil
IM	Intersil
INS	National Semiconductor
KMM	Texas Instruments
LF	National Semiconductor
LM	Signetics
LM	Texas Instruments
LS	Texas Instruments
NM	National Semiconductor
M	Mitsubishi
MAB	Mullard
MBL	Fujitsu
MC	Motorola
MC	Signetics
MC	Texas Instruments
MJ	Plessey
MK	Mostek
ML	Plessey
MM	National Semiconductor
MN	Plessey
MP	MPS
MSM	OKI
MV	Plessey
N	Signetics
NE	Signetics
NJ	Plessey
NS	National Semiconductor
NSC	National Semiconductor
P	AMD
P	Intel
PC	Signetics
PCF	Signetics

PIC	Plessey
R	Rockwell
R	Raytheon
RAY	Raytheon
RC	Raytheon
S	American Microsystems
SAA	Signetics
SCB	Signetics
SCN	Signetics
SCP	Solid State Scientific
SE	Signetics
SL	Plessey
SN	Texas Instruments
SP	Plessey
SY	Synertek
TAB	Plessey
TCA	Signetics
TCM	Texas Instruments
TDA	Signetics
TEA	Signetics
TIC	Texas Instruments
TIL	Texas Instruments
TIM	Texas Instruments
TIP	Texas Instruments
TL	Texas Instruments
TLC	Texas Instruments
TMM	Toshiba
TMP	Texas Instruments
TMS	Texas Instruments
UA	Signetics
UA	Texas Instruments
UCN	Sprague
UDN	Sprague
UDN	Texas Instruments
UGN	Sprague
ULN	Signetics
ULN	Sprague
ULN	Texas Instruments
UPB	NEC
UPD	NEC
X	Xicor
Z	Zilog
Z	SGS
ZN	Ferranti
μPD	NEC

CCITT recommendations

The International Telegraph and Telephone Consultative Committee (CCITT) produces internationally agreed standards for telecomunications. These standards appear as a number of recommendations which cover telecommunications apparatus and the transmission of both analogue and digital signals.

The International Telecommunications Union (ITU) is the parent body for the CCITT and is itself organised by and responsible to the United Nations.

The major CCITT recommendations are organised into series

which deal with data transmission over telephone circuits (V-series recommendations), data networks (X-series recommendations), digital networks (G-series recommendations), and integrated services digital networks (I-series recommendations).

CCITT publishes recommendations at approximately yearly intervals. A set of volumes (known collectively as the 'Red Book') contain the recommendations of the Eighth Plenary Assembly (1984). Volume VIII of the 'Red Book' contains seven sections which deal with data communication over the telephone network (V-series recommendations).

CCITT G-series recommendations

The following CCITT G-series recommendations relate to transmission systems and multiplexing equipment characteristics of digital networks:

G.701 General structure of the G.700, G.800 and G.800 recommendations

G.702 Terminology used for pulse code modulation (PCM) and digital transmission

G.703 General aspects of interfaces

G.704 Maintenance of digital networks

G.705 Integrated services digital networks (ISDN)

G.711 Pulse code modulation (PCM) of voice frequencies

G.712 Performance characteristics of PCM channels at audio frequencies

G.721 Hypothetical reference digital paths

G.722 Interconnection of digital paths using different techniques

G.731 Primary PCM multiplex equipment for voice frequencies

G.732 Characteristic of primary PCM multiplex equipment operating at 2048 kbps

G.733 Characteristics of primary PCM multiplex equipment operating at 1544 kbps

G.734 Frame structure for use with digital exchanges at 2048 kbps

G.735 Termination of 1544 kbps digital paths on digital exchanges

G.736 Characteristics of synchronous digital multiplex equipment operating at 1544 kbps

G.737 Characteristics of primary PCM multiplex equipment operating at 2048 kbps and offering synchronous 64 kbps digital access options

G.738 Characteristics of synchronous digital multiplex equipment operating at 2048 kbps

G.739 Characteristics of external access equipment operating at 2048 kbps and offering synchronous digital access at 64 kbps

G.741 General considerations on second order multiplex equipments

G.742 Second order digital multiplex equipment operating at 8448 kbps and using positive justification

G.743 Second order digital multiplex equipment operating at 6312 kbps and using positive justification

G.744 Second order PCM multiplex equipment operating at 8448 kbps

G.745 Second order digital multiplex equipment operating at 8448 kbps and using positive/zero/negative justification

G.746 Frame structure for use with digital exchanges at 8448 kbps

G.751 Digital multiplex equipment operating at third order bit rates of 34 368 kbps and fourth order bit rates of 139 264 kbps and using positive justification

G.752 Characteristics of digital multiplex equipment based on second order bit rates of 6312 kbps and using positive justification

CCITT I-series recommendations

The following CCITT I-series recommendations relate to integrated services digital networks (ISDNs):

CCITT V-series recommendations

The following CCITT V-series recommendations cover data transmission over the telephone network:

V.1	Equivalence between binary notation symbols and the significant conditions of a two condition code
V.2	Power levels for data transmission over telephone lines
V.3	International alphabet no. 5
V.4	General structure of signals of international alphabet no. 5 code for data transmission over public telephone networks
V.5	Standards of modulation rates and data signalling rates for synchronous data transmission in the general switched network
V.6	Standards of modulation rates and data signalling rates for synchronous data transmission on leased telephone-type circuits
V.7	Definitions of terms concerning data transmission over the telephone network
V.10	Electrical characteristics for unbalanced double-current interchange circuits for general use with integrated circuit equipment in the field of data communications (RS-423)
V.11	Electrical characteristics for balanced double-current interchange circuits for general use with integrated circuit equipment in the field of data communications (RS-422)
V.13	Answerback unit simulator
V.15	Use of acoustic coupling for data transmission
V.16	Recommendations for modems for the transmission of medical dialogue data
V.19	Modems for parallel data transmission using signalling frequencies
V.20	Parallel data transmission modems standardised for universal use in the general switched network
V.21	200 bps modem standardised for use in the switched telephone network
V.22	1200 bps full-duplex 2-wire modem standardised for use in the general switched telephone network and on leased lines
V.22 bis	2400 bps full-duplex 2-wire modem using frequency division techniques standardised for use in the general switched telephone network
V.23	600/1200 bps modem standardised for use in the general switched telephone network
V.24	List of definitions for interchange circuits between data terminal equipment and data circuit-terminating equipment (RS-232C)
V.25	Automatic calling and/or answering equipment on the general switched telephone network including disabling echo-suppressors on manually established calls
V.25 bis	Automatic calling and/or answering equipment on the general switched telephone network using the 100 series interchange circuits
V.26	2400 bps modem for use on 4-wire leased point-to-point leased telephone circuits
V.26 bis	2400/1200 bps modem standardised for use in the general switched telephone network
V.26 ter	2400 bps duplex modem using echo cancellation standardised for use in the general switched telephone

	network and on point-to-point 2-wire leased telephone circuits
V.27	4800 bps modem with manual equaliser standardised for use on leased telephone circuits
V.27 bis	4800/2400 bps modem with automatic equaliser standardised for use on leased circuits
V.27 ter	4800/2400 bps modem with automatic equaliser standardised for use in the general swtiched telephone network
V.28	Electrical characteristics for unbalanced double-current interchange circuits
V.29	9600 bps modem standardised for use on leased circuits
V.31	Electrical characteristics for single-current interchange circuits controlled by contact closure
V.32	Duplex modems operating at data rates of up to 9600 bps standardised for use in the general switched telephone network and in 2-wire leased telephone circuits
V.33	Full duplex synchronous or asynchronous transmission at 14.4 kbps for use in the public telephone network
V.35	Interface between DTE and DCE using electrical signals defined in V.11 (RS-449)
V.36	Modems for synchronous data transmission using 60–108 kHz group band circuits
V.37	Synchronous data transmission at date rates in excess of 72 kbps using 60–108 kHz group band circuits
V.40	Error indication with electromagnetic equipment
V.41	Code-independent error control system
V.50	Standard limits for transmission quality of data transmission
V.51	Organisation of the maintenance of international telephone-type circuits used for data transmission
V.52	Characteristics of distortion and error rate measuring apparatus for data transmission
V.53	Limits for the maintenance of telephone-type circuits used for data transmission
V.54	Loop test devices for modems
V.55	Specification for an impulsive noise measuring instrument for telephone-type circuits
V.56	Comparative tests for modems for use over telephone-type circuits
V.57	Comprehensive data test set for high signalling rates
V.110	Support of DTEs with V-series type interfaces by an ISDN (I.463)

CCITT X-series recommendations

The following CCITT X-series recommendations cover public data networks:

X.1	International user classes of service in public data networks and ISDN
X.2	International user facilities in public data networks
X.3	Packet assembly/disassembly facility in a public data network
X.4	General structure of signals of international alphabet no. 5 code for data transmission over public data networks
X.15	Definitions of terms concerning public data networks
X.20	Interface between data terminal equipment and data circuit-terminating equipment for start-stop transmission services on public data networks
X.20 bis	V21-compatible interface between data terminal

equipment and data circuit-terminating equipment for start-stop transmission services on public data networks

X.21 General-purpose interface between data terminal equipment and data circuit-terminating equipment for synchronous operation on public data networks

X.21 bis Use on public data networks of data terminal equipments which are designed for interfacing to synchronous V-series modems

X.22 Multiplex data terminal equipment/data circuit-terminating equipment for user classes 3–6

X.24 List of definitions of interchange circuits between data terminal equipment and data circuit-terminating equipment on public data networks

X.25 Interface between data terminal equipment and data circuit-terminating equipment for terminals operating in the packet mode on public data networks

X.26 Electrical characteristics for unbalanced double-current interchange circuits for general use with integrated circuit equipment in the field of data communications (identical to V.10)

X.27 Electrical characteristics for balanced double-current interchange circuits for general use with integrated circuit equipment in the field of data communications (identical to V.11)

X.28 Data terminal equipment/data circuit-terminating equipment interface for a start/stop mode data terminal equipment accessing the packet assembly/disassembly facility on a public data network situated in the same country

X.29 Procedures for exchange of control information and user data between a packet mode data circuit-terminating equipment and a packet assembly/disassembly facility

X.30 Support of X.21 and X.21 bis based data terminal equipment by an ISDN (I.461)

X.31 Support of packet mode terminal equipment by an ISDN (I.462)

X.32 Interface between data terminal equipment and data circuit-terminating equipment for terminals operating in packet mode and accessing a packet switched public data network through a public switched network.

X.50 Fundamental parameters of a multiplexing scheme for the international interface between synchronous data networks

X.50 bis Fundamental parameters of a 48 kbps user data signalling rate transmission scheme for the international interface between synchronous data networks

X.51 Fundamental parameters of a multiplexing scheme for the international interface between synchronous data networks using 10-bit envelope structure

X.51 bis Fundamental parameters of a 48 kbps user data signalling rate transmission scheme for the international interface between synchronous data networks using 10-bit envelope structure

X.52 Method of encoding asynchronous signals into a synchronous user bearer

X.53 Number of channels on international multiplex links at 64 kbps

X.54 Allocations of channels on international multiplex links at 64 kbps

X.60	Common channel signalling for circuit-switched data applications
X.61	Signalling system no. 7 (data user part)
X.70	Terminal and transit control signalling system on international circuits between asynchronous data networks
X.71	Decentralised terminal and transit control signalling system on international circuits between synchronous data networks
X.75	Terminal and transit call control procedures and data transfer systems on international circuits between packet-switched data networks
X.80	Interworking of inter-exchange signalling systems for circuit switched data services
X.87	Principles and procedures for realisation of international test facilities and network utilities in public data networks
X.92	Hypothetical reference connections for public synchronous data networks
X.95	Network parameters in public data networks
X.96	Call progress signals in public data networks
X.110	Routing principles for international public data services through switched public data networks of the same type
X.121	International numbering plan for public data networks
X.130	Provisional objectives for call set-up and clear-down times in public synchronous data networks (circuit-switching)
X.132	Provisional objectives for grade of service in international data communications over circuit-switched public data networks
X.150	Data terminal equipment and data circuit-terminating equipment test loops for public data networks
X.180	Administration arrangements for international closed user groups

The following CCITT X-series recommendations relate to data communications networks for open system interconnection (OSI):

X.200	Reference model of OSI for CCITT applications
X.210	OSI layer service definition conventions
X.213	Network service definition for OSI for CCITT applications
X.214	Transport service definition for OSI for CCITT applications
X.215	Session service definition for OSI for CCITT applications
X.224	Transport protocol specification for OSI for CCITT applications
X.225	Session protocol specification for OSI for CCITT applications
X.244	Procedure for the exchange of protocol identical during virtual call establishment on packet-switched public data networks
X.250	Formal description techniques for data communications protocols and services
X.400	Message handling service for all test communications and electronic mail

Note: The words *bis* and *ter* refer to the second and third parts of the relevant CCITT recommendation and these are usually concerned with enhancements to the original specification.

International alphabet no. 2 (IA2)

Position 12345	Letters shift enabled	Figures shift enabled
●●	A	–
● ●●	B	?
●●●	C	:
● ●	D	who are you?
●	E	3
● ●●	F	
● ●●	G	
● ●	H	
●●	I	8
●● ●	J	Bell
●●●●	K	(
● ●	L	)
●●●	M	.
●●	N	,
●●	O	9
●● ●	P	0
●●● ●	Q	1
● ●	R	4
● ●	S	!
●	T	5
●●●	U	7
●●●●	V	=
●● ●	W	2
● ●●●	X	/
● ● ●	Y	6
● ●	Z	+
		Blank
●●●●●		Letters shift
●● ●●		Figure shift
●		Space
●		Carriage return
●		Line feed

Notes:

1. ● = punched holes in paper tape media
2. Sprocket feed holes are located between positions 2 and 3 on paper tape media.

Extended binary coded decimal interchange code (EBCDIC)

24 Extended binary coded decimal interchange code (EBCDIC)

EBCDIC standard code table

									Most significant bits							
b3 b2 b1 b0 / **b7 b6 b5 b4**	0000	0001	0010	0011	0100	0101	0110	0111	1000	1001	1010	1011	1100	1101	1110	1111
row / **col**	0	1	2	3	4	5	6	7	8	9	10	11	12	13	14	15
0000 — 0	NULL				SP	&	-									0
0001 — 1							/		a	j			A	J		1
0010 — 2									b	k	s		B	K	S	2
0011 — 3									c	l	t		C	L	T	3
0100 — 4	PF	RES	BYP	PN					d	m	u		D	M	U	4
0101 — 5	HT	NL	LF	RS					e	n	v		E	N	V	5
0110 — 6	LC	BS	EOB	UC					f	o	w		F	O	W	6
0111 — 7	DEL	IL	PRE	EOT					g	p	x		G	P	X	7
1000 — 8									h	q	y		H	Q	Y	8
1001 — 9									i	r	z		I	R	Z	9
1010 — 10			SM		¢	!	¦	:								
1011 — 11					.	$	,	#								
1100 — 12					<	*	%	@								
1101 — 13					(	)	_	'								
1110 — 14					+	;	>	=								
1111 — 15					|	¬	?	"								

Least significant bits

EBCDIC control characters

Character	Full name
BS	Backspace
BYP	Bypass
DEL	Delete
EOB	End of block
EOT	End of transmission
HT	Horizontal tab
IL	Idle
LC	Lower case
LF	Line feed
NL	New line
NULL	Null/idle
PF	Punch off
PN	Punch on
PRE	Prefix
RES	Restore
RS	Reader stop
SM	Set mode
SP	Space
UC	Upper case

International alphabet no. 5 (IA5)

IA5 standard code table

			Most significant bits							
		$b_6b_5b_4$	000	001	010	011	100	101	110	111
$b_3b_2b_1b_0$	row	col	0	1	2	3	4	5	6	7
0000	0		NUL	DLE	SP	0	@	P		p
0001	1		SOH	DC1	!	1	A	Q	a	q
0010	2		STX	DC2	"	2	B	R	b	r
0011	3		ETX	DC3	£/#	3	C	S	c	s
0100	4		EOT	DC4	$	4	D	T	d	t
0101	5		ENQ	NAK	%	5	E	U	e	u
0110	6		ACK	SYN	&	6	F	V	f	v
0111	7		BEL	ETB	'	7	G	W	g	w
1000	8		BS	CAN	(	8	H	X	h	x
1001	9		HT	EM	)	9	I	Y	i	y
1010	10		LF	SUB	*	:	J	Z	j	z
1011	11		VT	ESC	+	;	K	[	k	{
1100	12		FF	FS	,	<	L	\	l	:
1101	13		CR	GS	−	=	M	]	m	}
1110	14		SO	RS	.	>	N	ˆ	n	˜
1111	15		SI	US	/	?	O	_	o	DEL

Least significant bits

IA5 control characters

Character	Full name	Function

(a) Logical communication control

ACK	acknowledge	indicates an affirmative response (transmitted by a receiver to acknowledge that data has been received without error)
DLE	data link escape	marks the start of a contiguous sequence of characters which provide supplementary data transmission control functions (only graphics and transmission control characters appear in DLE sequences)
ENQ	enquiry	requests a response from a remote station which may either take the form of a station identification or status (the first use of ENQ after a connection has been established is equivalent to "who are you?")
EOT	end of trans-mission	concludes the transmission (and may also terminate communications by turning a device off)
ETB	end of trans-mission block	indicates the end of a transmission block (unrelated to any division in the format of the logical data itself)
ETX	end of text	indicates the last character in the transmission of text (often generated by means of CTRL-C in many terminals)
NAK	negative acknowledge	indicates a negative response (the opposite of ACK)
SOH	start of heading	indicates the first character of the heading of an information message
STX	start of text	terminates a heading and indicates that text follows
SYN	synchronous idle	provides a signal which may be needed to achieve (or retain) synchronisation between devices (used in the idle condition when no other characters are transmitted)

(b) Physical communication control

CAN	cancel	indicates that the preceding data is to be disregarded (it may contain errors). CAN is usually employed on a line-by-line basis such that, when CAN appears within a serial data stream, data is disregarded up to the last CR character received. On most

Character	Full name	Function
		terminals, CAN is generated by CTRL-X
DEL	delete	DEL was originally used to obliterate unwanted characters in punched tape. However, in applications where it will not affect the information content of a data stream, DEL may be used for media or time-fill (see note 1)
EM	end of medium	identifies the end of the used portion of the medium (not necessarily the physical end of the medium)
NUL	null	may be inserted into, or removed from, the data stream without affecting the information content (and may thus be used to accomplish media or time-fill)
SUB	substitute	may be used to replace a suspect character (ie one which is for one reason or another considered invalid)

(c) Device control

Character	Full name	Function
BEL	bell	produces an audible signal to attract the user's attention
BS	backspace	a layout character which moves the printing position backwards by one character print position (often generated by CTRL-H). With hardcopy devices, BS can be used for a variety of purposes including underlining, bold highlighting, and the generation of composite characters
CR	carriage return	a layout character which moves the printing position to the start of the *current* line
DC1-DC4	device control	used to enabled or disable additional facilities which may be available at the receiver (often used to control specialised printing functions)
FF	form feed	a layout character which moves the printing position to the first printing line on the next page (form)
HT	horizontal tabulation	a layout character which moves the printing position to the next in a series of predefined horizontal printing positions (horizontal tab settings)
LF	line feed	a layout character which moves the printing position to the next printing line. In some equipment,

Character	Full name	Function
		LF is sometimes combined with CR so that the print position is moved to the start of the *next* line. To avoid confusion, LF is sometimes referred to as NL (or new line)
VT	vertical tabulation	a layout character which moves the printing position to the next in a series of predefined vertical printing positions (vertical tab. settings). Depending upon the current vertical tab. setting, VT is equivalent to one, or more, LF characters.

(d) Formatting and string processing (see note 2)

FS	field separator	terminates a file information block
GS	group separator	terminates a group information block
RS	record separator	terminates a record information block
US	unit separator	terminates a unit information block

(e) Character/graphic set control

ESC	escape	used to modify or extend the standard character set. The escape character changes the meaning of the character which follows according to some previously defined scheme. NUL, DEL communication control characters must not be used in defining escape sequences
SI	shift-in	characters which follow SI should be interpreted according to the standard code table
SO	shift-out	characters which follow SO should be interpreted as being outside the standard code table. The meaning of the control characters from columns 0 and 1 are, however, preserved.

Notes:

1. Note that DEL, unlike other control characters which occupy columns 0 and 1, is in column 7 (all bits of the code for DEL are set to logic 1)
2. Information block separators have the following heirarchy (arranged in ascending order): US, RS, GS, FS. Also note that information blocks may not themselves be divided by separators of higher order.

Representative teletype keyboard layout (IA2)

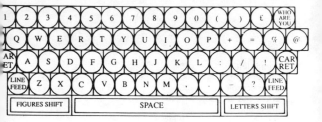

Representative personal computer keyboard layout

Terminal control codes

Control code sequences are used by terminals to provide special functions such as deletion of the character at the cursor position, clearing the entire screen display, and horizontal tabulation. In addition, special function keys or keypads may be provided and these also produce control code sequences (often beginning with the ASCII ESCape character (1B hex). The following is a list of the control code sequences used in some of the most popular computer terminals:

ADDS Viewpoint

Key	Control code sequence (hexadecimal)
Horizontal tab	09
Insert character	1B,46
Insert line	1B,4D
Delete character	1B,45
Delete line	1B,6C
Home cursor	1B,59,5F,5F
Cursor up	01
Cursor down	0A

Key	Control code sequence (hexadecimal)
Cursor left	15
Cursor right	06
Clear screen	0C
Erase end of line	1B,4B
Erase end of screen	1B,6B
Function 1 (F1)	02,31,0D
Function 2 (F2)	02,32,0D
Function 3 (F3)	02,33,0D
Function 4 (F4)	02,34,0D
Function 5 (F5)	02,35,0D
Function 6 (F6)	02,36,0D
Function 7 (F7)	02,37,0D
Function 8 (F8)	02,38,0D
Shift function 1 (F1)	02,19,0D
Shift function 2 (F2)	02,29,0D
Shift function 3 (F3)	02,39,0D
Shift function 4 (F4)	02,49,0D
Shift function 5 (F5)	02,59,0D
Shift function 6 (F6)	02,69,0D
Shift function 7 (F7)	02,79,0D
Shift function 8 (F8)	02,89,0D

Heath/Zenith 19

Key	Control code sequence (hexadecimal)
Horizontal tab	09
Insert line	1B,4C
Delete line	1B,4D
Home cursor	1B,59,5F,5F
Cursor up	1B,41
Cursor down	1B,42
Cursor left	1B,44
Cursor right	1B,43
Erase end of line	1B,45
Program function 1 (PF1)	1B,53
Program function 2 (PF2)	1B,54
Program function 3 (PF3)	1B,55
Program function 4 (PF4)	1B,56
Program function 5 (PF5)	1B,57
Program function 6 (PF6)	1B,50
Program function 7 (PF7)	1B,51
Program function 8 (PF8)	1B,52
Program function 9 (PF9)	1B,30
Program function 10 (PF10)	1B,31

IBM 3101

Key	Control code sequence (hexadecimal)
Horizontal tab	09
Character delete	7F
Home cursor	1B,48
Cursor up	1B,41
Cursor down	1B,42
Cursor left	1B,44
Cursor right	1B,43
Clear screen	1B,4C
Erase end of line	1B,49
Erase end of screen	1B,4A
Program function 1 (PF1)	1B,61,0D
Program function 2 (PF2)	1B,62,0D
Program function 3 (PF3)	1B,63,0D
Program function 4 (PF4)	1B,64,0D
Program function 5 (PF5)	1B,65,0D
Program function 6 (PF6)	1B,66,0D
Program function 7 (PF7)	1B,67,0D
Program function 8 (PF8)	1B,68,0D

Lear Siegler ADM 3/5

Key	Control code sequence (hexadecimal)
Horizontal tab	1B,49
Reverse tab	1B,51
Home cursor	1E
Cursor up	1B
Cursor down	0A
Cursor left	18
Cursor right	1C
Clear screen	1A
Erase end of line	1B,54

Televideo 910/920

Key	Control code sequence (hexadecimal)
Horizontal tab	09
Reverse tab	1B,49
Insert character	1B,51

Key	Control code sequence (hexadecimal)
Insert line	1B,45
Delete character	1B,57
Delete line	1B,52
Home cursor	1E
Cursor up	1B
Cursor down	0A
Cursor left	18
Cursor right	1C
Clear screen	1A
Line erase	1B,54
Page erase	1B,59
Function 1 (PF1)	01,40,0D
Function 2 (PF2)	01,41,0D
Function 3 (PF3)	01,42,0D
Function 4 (PF4)	01,43,0D
Function 5 (PF5)	01,44,0D
Function 6 (PF6)	01,45,0D
Function 7 (PF7)	01,46,0D
Function 8 (PF8)	01,47,0D
Function 9 (PF9)	01,48,0D
Function 10 (PF10)	01,49,0D
Function 11 (PF11)	01,4A,0D
Shift line erase	1B,74
Shift page erase	1B,79
Shift line insert	1B,4E
Shift line delete	1B,4F
Shift character insert	1B,71
Shift character delete	1B,72
Function	01,nn,0D

Televideo 925/950

Key	Control code sequence (hexadecimal)
Horizontal tab	09
Reverse tab	1B,49
Insert character	1B,51
Insert line	1B,45
Delete character	1B,57
Delete line	1B,52
Home cursor	1E
Cursor up	1B
Cursor down	16
Cursor left	18
Cursor right	1C
Clear screen	1A
Line erase	1B,54

Key	Control code sequence (hexadecimal)
Page erase	1B,59
Function 1 (PF1)	01,40,0D
Function 2 (PF2)	01,41,0D
Function 3 (PF3)	01,42,0D
Function 4 (PF4)	01,43,0D
Function 5 (PF5)	01,44,0D
Function 6 (PF6)	01,45,0D
Function 7 (PF7)	01,46,0D
Function 8 (PF8)	01,47,0D
Function 9 (PF9)	01,48,0D
Function 10 (PF10)	01,49,0D
Function 11 (PF11)	01,4A,0D
Shift line erase	1B,74
Shift page erase	1B,79
Shift line insert	1B,4E
Shift line delete	1B,4F
Shift character insert	1B,71
Shift character delete	1B,72
Function	01,nn,0D

VT-52

Key	Control code sequence (hexadecimal)
Horizontal tab	09
Character delete	7F
Home cursor	1B,48
Cursor up	1B,41
Cursor down	1B,42
Cursor left	1B,44
Cursor right	1B,43
Clear screen	1B,48,1B,4A
Erase end of line	1B,4B
Keypad application mode 0	1B,3F,70
Keypad application mode 1	1B,3F,71
Keypad application mode 2	1B,3F,72
Keypad application mode 3	1B,3F,73
Keypad application mode 4	1B,3F,74
Keypad application mode 5	1B,3F,75
Keypad application mode 6	1B,3F,76
Keypad application mode 7	1B,3F,77
Keypad application mode 8	1B,3F,78
Keypad application mode 9	1B,3F,79
Keypad application mode -	1B,3F,6D
Keypad application mode ,	1B,3F,6C
Keypad application mode .	1B,3F,6E
Keypad application mode ENTER	1B,3F,4D

Key	Control code sequence (hexadecimal)
Program function 1 (PF1)	1B,50
Program function 2 (PF2)	1B,51
Program function 3 (PF3)	1B,52
Program function 4 (PF4)	1B,53

VT-100

Key	Control code sequence (hexadecimal)
Horizontal tab	09
Character delete	7F
Home cursor	1B,5B,48
Cursor up	1B,5B,41
Cursor down	1B,5B,42
Cursor left	1B,5B,44
Cursor right	1B,5B,43
Clear screen	1B,5B,48,1B,5B,32,4A
Erase end of line	1B,5B,4B
Insert line	1B,5B,4C
Delete line	1B,5B,4D
Line feed	0A
Keypad application mode 0	1B,4F,70
Keypad application mode 1	1B,4F,71
Keypad application mode 2	1B,4F,72
Keypad application mode 3	1B,4F,73
Keypad application mode 4	1B,4F,74
Keypad application mode 5	1B,4F,75
Keypad application mode 6	1B,4F,76
Keypad application mode 7	1B,4F,77
Keypad application mode 8	1B,4F,78
Keypad application mode 9	1B,4F,79
Keypad application mode -	1B,4F,6D
Keypad application mode ,	1B,4F,6C
Keypad application mode .	1B,4F,6E
Keypad application mode ENTER	1B,4F,4D
Program function 1 (PF1)	1B,4F,50
Program function 2 (PF2)	1B,4F,51
Program function 3 (PF3)	1B,4F,52
Program function 4 (PF4)	1B,4F,53

WYSE 100

Key	Control code sequence (hexadecimal)
Horizontal tab	09
Reverse tab	1B,49
Insert character	1B,51
Insert line	1B,45
Delete character	7F
Delete line	1B,52
Home cursor	1E
Cursor up	1B
Cursor down	0A
Cursor left	18
Cursor right	1C
Clear screen	1A
Line erase	1B,54
Page erase	1B,59
Function 1 (F1)	01,40,0D
Function 2 (F2)	01,41,0D
Function 3 (F3)	01,42,0D
Function 4 (F4)	01,43,0D
Function 5 (F5)	01,44,0D
Function 6 (F6)	01,45,0D
Function 7 (F7)	01,46,0D
Function 8 (F8)	01,47,0D
Shift function 1 (F1)	01,48,0D
Shift function 2 (F2)	01,49,0D
Shift function 3 (F3)	01,4A,0D
Shift function 4 (F4)	01,4B,0D
Shift function 5 (F5)	01,4C,0D
Shift function 6 (F6)	01,4D,0D
Shift function 7 (F7)	01,4E,0D
Shift function 8 (F8)	01,4F,0D

Commonly used control characters (with keyboard entry)

Keyboard	Decimal	Binary	Hexadecimal	ASCII	Function (eg, MS-DOS)
CTRL-@	0	00000000	00	NUL	
CTRL-A	1	00000001	01	SOH	
CTRL-B	2	00000010	02	STX	
CTRL-C	3	00000011	03	ETX	Cancels (if possible) the current process or aborts the current program (ie, same affect as CTRL-BREAK)

Keyboard	Decimal	Binary	Hexadecimal	ASCII	Function (eg. MS-DOS)
CTRL-D	4	00000100	04	EOT	
CTRL-E	5	00000101	05	ENQ	
CTRL-F	6	00000110	06	ACK	
CTRL-G	7	00000111	07	BEL	Bell (not normally executable directly from the keyboard)
CTRL-H	8	00001000	08	BS	Backspace (same as BS or left arrow keys)
CTRL-I	9	00001001	09	HT	Tab (usually eight print positions to the right). Same affect as TAB key
CTRL-J	10	00001010	0A	LF	Line feed. Moves the print position to the next line. Same effect as CTRL-RETURN
CTRL-K	11	00001011	0B	VT	
CTRL-L	12	00001100	0C	FF	Form feed. Moves the print position to the corresponding point on the next page/form
CTRL-M	13	00001101	0D	CR	Carriage return. Same effect as the RETURN key
CTRL-N	14	00001110	0E	SO	Enables expanded mode printing (EPSON)
CTRL-O	15	00001111	0F	SI	Enables condensed mode printing (EPSON)
CTRL-P	16	00010000	10	DLE	Print. Toggles (on or off) the echoing of characters printed on the screen to a line printer. Same effect as CTRL-PRT SCN
CTRL-Q	17	00010001	11	DC1	X-ON (resumes flow)
CTRL-R	18	00010010	12	DC2	Disables condensed mode printing (EPSON)
CTRL-S	19	00010011	13	DC3	X-OFF (halts flow). May be used to interrupt flow of characters when a TYPE command is being executed
CTRL-T	20	00010100	14	DC4	Disables expanded mode printing (EPSON)
CTRL-U	21	00010101	15	NAK	
CTRL-V	22	00010110	16	SYN	
CTRL-W	23	00010111	17	ETB	
CTRL-X	24	00011000	18	CAN	Cancel text in buffer (EPSON)
CTRL-Y	25	00011001	19	EM	
CTRL-Z	26	00011010	1A	SUB	End-of-file (EOF)
CTRL-[	27	00011011	1B	ESC	Escape (same effect as an ESC key)
CTRL-\	28	00011100	1C	FS	
CTRL-]	29	00011101	1D	GS	

Keyboard	Decimal	Binary	Hexadecimal	ASCII	Function (eg, MS-DOS)
CTRL-^	30	00011110	1E	RS	
CTRL-__	31	00011111	1F	US	
SPACE	32	00100000	20	SP	Generated by the space bar.

Notes:

1. CTRL is often represented by the character '^'. Hence CTRL-A (control-A) may be shown as ^A
2. When entering control characters from a keyboard, the control key (CTRL) must be held down *before* the other keyboard character is depressed
3. Control characters can usually be incorporated in BASIC programs by using statements of the form: (L)PRINT CHR$(n). To produce condensed mode printing on an EPSON printer, for example, the following BASIC statement is used: LPRINT CHR$(15).

Decimal, binary, hexadecimal and ASCII conversion table

Decimal	Binary	Hexadecimal	ASCII
0	00000000	00	NUL
1	00000001	01	SOH
2	00000010	02	STX
3	00000011	03	ETX
4	00000100	04	EOT
5	00000101	05	ENQ
6	00000110	06	ACK
7	00000111	07	BEL
8	00001000	08	BS
9	00001001	09	HT
10	00001010	0A	LF
11	00001011	0B	VT
12	00001100	0C	FF
13	00001101	0D	CR
14	00001110	0E	SO
15	00001111	0F	SI
16	00010000	10	DLE
17	00010001	11	DC1
18	00010010	12	DC2
19	00010011	13	DC3
20	00010100	14	DC4
21	00010101	15	NAK
22	00010110	16	SYN
23	00010111	17	ETB
24	00011000	18	CAN
25	00011001	19	EM
26	00011010	1A	SUB

Decimal	Binary	Hexadecimal	ASCII
27	00011011	1B	ESC
28	00011100	1C	FS
29	00011101	1D	GS
30	00011110	1E	RS
31	00011111	1F	US
32	00100000	20	SP
33	00100001	21	!
34	00100010	22	"
35	00100011	23	#
36	00100100	24	$
37	00100101	25	%
38	00100110	26	&
39	00100111	27	'
40	00101000	28	(
41	00101001	29	)
42	00101010	2A	*
43	00101011	2B	+
44	00101100	2C	,
45	00101101	2D	–
46	00101110	2E	.
47	00101111	2F	/
48	00110000	30	0
49	00110001	31	1
50	00110010	32	2
51	00110011	33	3
52	00110100	34	4
53	00110101	35	5
54	00110110	36	6
55	00110111	37	7
56	00111000	38	8
57	00111001	39	9
58	00111010	3A	:
59	00111011	3B	;
60	00111100	3C	<
61	00111101	3D	=
62	00111110	3E	>
63	00111111	3F	?
64	01000000	40	@
65	01000001	41	A
66	01000010	42	B
67	01000011	43	C
68	01000100	44	D
69	01000101	45	E
70	01000110	46	F
71	01000111	47	G
72	01001000	48	H
73	01001001	49	I
74	01001010	4A	J
75	01001011	4B	K
76	01001100	4C	L
77	01001101	4D	M
78	01001110	4E	N
79	01001111	4F	O
80	01010000	50	P

Decimal	Binary	Hexadecimal	ASCII
81	01010001	51	Q
82	01010010	52	R
83	01010011	53	S
84	01010100	54	T
85	01010101	55	U
86	01010110	56	V
87	01010111	57	W
88	01011000	58	X
89	01011001	59	Y
90	01011010	5A	Z
91	01011011	5B	[
92	01011100	5C	\
93	01011101	5D	]
94	01011110	5E	^
95	01011111	5F	_
96	01100000	60	`
97	01100001	61	a
98	01100010	62	b
99	01100011	63	c
100	01100100	64	d
101	01100101	65	e
102	01100110	66	f
103	01100111	67	g
104	01101000	68	h
105	01101001	69	i
106	01101010	6A	j
107	01101011	6B	k
108	01101100	6C	l
109	01101101	6D	m
110	01101110	6E	n
111	01101111	6F	o
112	01110000	70	p
113	01110001	71	q
114	01110010	72	r
115	01110011	73	s
116	01110100	74	t
117	01110101	75	u
118	01110110	76	v
119	01110111	77	w
120	01111000	78	x
121	01111001	79	y
122	01111010	7A	z
123	01111011	7B	{
124	01111100	7C	:
125	01111101	7D	}
126	01111110	7E	~
127	01111111	7F	DEL
128	10000000	80	
129	10000001	81	
130	10000010	82	
131	10000011	83	
132	10000100	84	
133	10000101	85	
134	10000110	86	

Decimal	Binary	Hexadecimal
135	10000111	87
136	10001000	88
137	10001001	89
138	10001010	8A
139	10001011	8B
140	10001100	8C
141	10001101	8D
142	10001110	8E
143	10001111	8F
144	10010000	90
145	10010001	91
146	10010010	92
147	10010011	93
148	10010100	94
149	10010101	95
150	10010110	96
151	10010111	97
152	10011000	98
153	10011001	99
154	10011010	9A
155	10011011	9B
156	10011100	9C
157	10011101	9D
158	10011110	9E
159	10011111	9F
160	10100000	A0
161	10100001	A1
162	10100010	A2
163	10100011	A3
164	10100100	A4
165	10100101	A5
166	10100110	A6
167	10100111	A7
168	10101000	A8
169	10101001	A9
170	10101010	AA
171	10101011	AB
172	10101100	AC
173	10101101	AD
174	10101110	AE
175	10101111	AF
176	10110000	B0
177	10110001	B1
178	10110010	B2
179	10110011	B3
180	10110100	B4
181	10110101	B5
182	10110110	B6
183	10110111	B7
184	10111000	B8
185	10111001	B9
186	10111010	BA
187	10111011	BB
188	10111100	BC

Decimal	Binary	Hexadecimal
189	10111101	BD
190	10111110	BE
191	10111111	BF
192	11000000	C0
193	11000001	C1
194	11000010	C2
195	11000011	C3
196	11000100	C4
197	11000101	C5
198	11000110	C6
199	11000111	C7
200	11001000	C8
201	11001001	C9
202	11001010	CA
203	11001011	CB
204	11001100	CC
205	11001101	CD
206	11001110	CE
207	11001111	CF
208	11010000	D0
209	11010001	D1
210	11010010	D2
211	11010011	D3
212	11010100	D4
213	11010101	D5
214	11010110	D6
215	11010111	D7
216	11011000	D8
217	11011001	D9
218	11011010	DA
219	11011011	DB
220	11011100	DC
221	11011101	DD
222	11011110	DE
223	11011111	DF
224	11100000	E0
225	11100001	E1
226	11100010	E2
227	11100011	E3
228	11100100	E4
229	11100101	E5
230	11100110	E6
231	11100111	E7
232	11101000	E8
233	11101001	E9
234	11101010	EA
235	11101011	EB
236	11101100	EC
237	11101101	ED
238	11101110	EE
239	11101111	EF
240	11110000	F0
241	11110001	F1
242	11110010	F2

Decimal	Binary	Hexadecimal
243	11110011	F3
244	11110100	F4
245	11110101	F5
246	11110110	F6
247	11110111	F7
248	11111000	F8
249	11111001	F9
250	11111010	FA
251	11111011	FB
252	11111100	FC
253	11111101	FD
254	11111110	FE
255	11111111	FF

Powers of 2

n	2^n
0	1
1	2
2	4
3	8
4	16
5	32
6	64
7	128
8	256
9	512
10	1024
11	2048
12	4096
13	8192
14	16384
15	32768
16	65536
17	131072
18	262144
19	524288
20	1048576
21	2097152
22	4194304
23	8388608
24	16777216
25	33554432
26	67108864
27	134217728
28	268435456
29	536870912
30	1073741824
31	2147483648
32	4294967296

Power of 16

n	16^n
0	1
1	16
2	256
3	4096
4	65536
5	1048576
6	16777216
7	268435456
8	4294967296

Parallel I/O devices

Parallel I/O devices allow a byte of data to be transferred at a time between computer systems and external devices. Parallel I/O is relatively easy to implement since it only requires an arrangement based on 8-bit buffers or latches. The software and hardware requirements of this form of I/O are thus minimal.

Parallel I/O devices enjoy a variety of names depending upon their manufacturer. Despite this, parallel I/O devices are remarkably similar in internal architecture and operation with only a few minor differences distinguishing one device from the next.

Programmable parallel I/O devices can normally be configured (under software control) in one of several modes:

(a) all eight lines configured as inputs
(b) all eight lines configured as outputs
(c) lines individually configured as inputs or outputs.

In addiiton, extra lines to I/O lines are normally available to facilitate *handshaking*. This provides a means of controlling the exchange of data between a computer system and external hardware. The nomenclature used for parallel I/O lines and their function tends to vary from chip to chip. The following applies to the majority of devices:

PA0 to PA7   Port A I/O lines; 0 corresponds to the least significant bit (LSB) whilst 7 corresponds to the most significant bit (MSB)

CA1 to CA2   Handshaking lines for Port A; CA1 is an interrupt input whilst CA2 can be used as both an interrupt input and peripheral control output

PB0 to PB7   Port B I/O lines; 0 corresponds to the least significant bit (LSB) whilst 7 corresponds to the most significant bit (MSB)

CB1 to CB2   Handshaking lines for Port B; CB1 is an interrupt input whilst CB2 can be used as both an interrupt input and peripheral control output.

Programmable I/O devices are invariably TTL-compatible and buffered to support at least one conventional TTL load. Several programmable parallel I/O devices have port output lines (usually the B group) which are able to source sufficient current to permit direct connection to the base of a conventional or Darlington-type transistor. This device can then be used as a relay or lamp driver. Alternatively, high-voltage open-collector octal drivers may be connected directly to the port output lines.

Internal architecture of a representative parallel I/O device

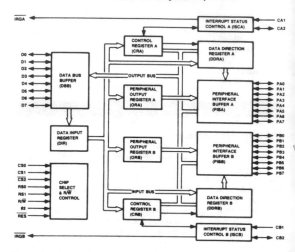

Internal registers of a typical programmable parallel I/O device

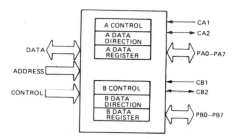

CPU interface to a programmable parallel I/O device

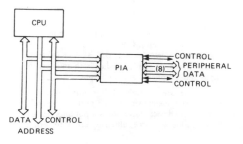

IEEE-488 interface standard

The IEEE-488 bus (also known as the Hewlett Packard instrument bus and the general-purpose instrument bus) provides a means of interconnecting a microcomputer controller with a vast range of test and measuring instruments. The bus is ideally suited to the implementation of automatic test equipment (ATE), and it has become increasingly popular in the last decade with a myriad of applications which range from routine production tests to the solution of highly complex and specialised measurement problems.

In the past, IEEE-488 facilities have tended to be available within only the more expensive test equipment. The necessary interface is, however, becoming increasingly commonplace in medium- and low-priced instruments. This trend reflects not only an increased demand from the test equipment user, but also the availability of low-cost dedicated IEEE-488 controller chips.

Nowadays, most items of modern electronic test equipment (such as digital voltmeters and signal generators) and many items of peripheral equipment are either fitted with the necessary IEEE-488 interface as standard or can be upgraded with optional IEEE-488 interface cards. This provision allows them to be connected to a microcomputer controller via the IEEE-488 bus so that the controller can be used both to supervise their operation and process the data which they collect.

IEEE-488 devices

The IEEE-488 standard provides for the following categories of device:

(a) Listeners
Listeners can receive data and control signals from other devices connected to the bus, but are not capable of generating data. An obvious example of a listener is a signal generator.

(b) Talkers
Talkers are only capable of placing data on the bus and cannot receive data. Typical examples of talkers are magnetic tape, magnetic stripe, and bar code readers. Note that, while only one talker can be active (ie, presenting data to the bus) at a given time, it is possible for a number of listeners to be active simultaneously (ie, receiving and/or processing the data).

(c) Talkers and listeners
The function of a talker and listener can be combined in a single instrument. Such instruments can both send data to and receive data from the bus. A digital multimeter is a typical example of a talker and listener. Data is sent to it in order to change ranges and is returned to the bus in the form of digitised readings of voltage, current, and resistance.

(d) Controllers
Controllers are used to supervise the flow of data on the bus and provide processing facilities. The controller within an IEEE-488

system is invariably a microcomputer and, whilst some manufacturers provide dedicated microprocessor based IEEE-488 controllers, this function is often provided by means of a PC or PC-compatible microcomputer.

IEEE-488 bus signals

The IEEE-488 bus uses eight multi-purpose bi-directional parallel data lines. These are used to transfer data, addresses, commands, and status bytes. In addition, five bus management and three handshake lines are provided.

The connector used for the IEEE-488 bus is invariably a 24-pin Amphenol type having the following pin assignment:

Pin number	Abbreviation	Function
1	DIO1	Data line 1
2	DIO2	Data line 2
3	DIO3	Data line 3
4	DIO4	Data line 4
5	EOI	End or identify. This signal is generated by a talker to indicate the last byte of data in a multi-byte data transfer. EOI is also issued by the active controller to perform a parallel poll by simultaneously asserting EOI and ATN.
6	DAV	Data valid. This signal is asserted by a talker to indicate that valid data has been placed on the bus.
7	NRFD	Not ready for data. This signal is asserted by a listener to indicate that it is not yet ready to accept data.
8	NDAC	Not data accepted. This signal is asserted by a listener whilst data is being accepted. When several devices are simultaneously listening, each device releases this line at its own rate (the slowest device will be the last to release the line).
9	IFC	Interface clear. Asserted by the controller in order to initialise the system in a known state.
10	SRQ	Service request. This signal is asserted by a device wishing to gain the attention of the controller. Note that this line employs wire-OR'd logic.
11	ATN	Attention. Asserted by the controller when placing a command on to the bus. When the line is asserted this indicates that the information placed by the controller on the data lines is to be interpreted as a command. When it is not asserted, information placed on the data lines by the

Pin number	Abbreviation	Function
		controller must be interpreted as data. ATN is always driven by the active controller.
12	SHIELD	Shield.
13	DIO5	Data line 5
14	DIO6	Date line 6
15	DIO7	Data line 7
16	DIO8	Data line 8
17	REN	Remote enable. This line is used to enable or disable bus control (thus permitting an instrument to be controlled from its own front panel rather than from the bus).
18–24	GND	Ground/common signal return.

Notes:
1. Handshake signals (DAV, NRFD, and NDAC) employ active low open-collector outputs which may be used in a wired-OR configuration.
2. All remaining signals are fully TTL compatible and are active low.

IEEE-488 bus connector

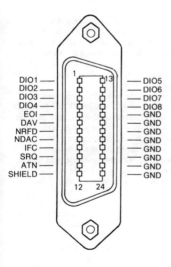

IEEE-488 commands
Bus commands are signalled by taking the ATN line low. Commands are then placed on the bus by the controller and directed to individual devices by placing a unique address on the lower five data bus lines. Alternatively, universal commands may be issued to all of the participating devices.

Handshaking

The IEEE-488 bus uses three handshake lines (DAV, NRFD, and NDAC). The handshake protocol adopted ensures that reliable data transfer occurs at a rate determined by the *slowest* listener.

A talker wishing to place data on the bus first ensures that NDAC is in a released state. This indicates that all of the listeners have accepted the previous data byte. The talker then places the byte on the bus and waits until NRFD is released. This indicates that all of the addressed listeners are ready to accept the data. Finally, the talker asserts DAV to indicate that the data on the bus is valid.

IEEE-488 handshake sequence

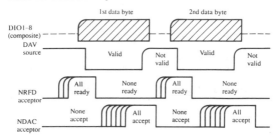

Service requests

The service request (SRQ) line is asserted whenever a device wishes to attract the attention of the active controller. SRQ essentially behaves as a shared interrupt line since all devices have common access to it. In order to determine which device has generated a service request, it is necessary for the controller to carry out a poll of the devices present. The polling process may be carried out either serially or in parallel.

In the case of *serial polling*, each device will respond to the controller by placing a status byte on the bus. DIO7 will be set if the device in question is requesting service, otherwise this data bit will be reset. The active controller continues to poll each device present in order to determine which one has generated the service request. The remaining bits within the status byte are used to indicate the status of a device and, once the controller has located the device which requires service, it is a fairly simple matter to determine its status and instigate the appropriate action.

In the case of *parallel polling*, each device asserts an individual data line. The controller can thus very quickly determine which device requires attention. The controller, however, cannot ascertain the status of the device which has generated the service request at the same time. In some cases it will be necessary, therefore, to carry out a subsequent serial poll of the same device in order to determine its status.

Multiline commands

The controller sends multiline commands over the bus as data bytes with ATN asserted. Multiline commands are divided into five groups, as follows:

Command group	Abbreviation	Function	Command byte
Addressed command	ACG	Used to select bus functions affecting listeners (eg, GTL which restores local front-panel control of an instrument)	00–0F
Universal command	UCG	Used to select bus functions which apply to all devices (eg, SPE which instructs all devices to output their serial poll status byte when they become the active talker)	10–1F

IEEE-488 command codes

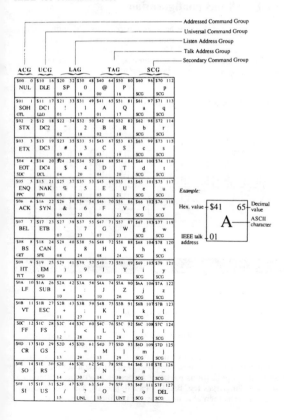

Example:

Hex value $41 → 65 Decimal value

A ← ASCII character

IEEE talk address $01

Addressed Command Group
Universal Command Group
Listen Address Group
Talk Address Group
Secondary Command Group

Command group	Abbreviation	Function	Command byte
Listen address	LAG	Sets a specified device to listen	20–3E
	UNL	Sets all devices to unlisten status	3F
Talk address	TAG	Sets a specified device to talk	40–5E
	UNL	Sets all devices to untalk status	5F
Secondary command	SCG	Used to specify a device sub-address or sub-function (also used in a parallel poll configure sequence)	60–7F

IEEE-488 bus configuration

Since the physical distance between devices is usually quite small (less than 20 m), data rates may be relatively fast. Data rates of between 50 kbytes s^{-1} and 250 kbyte s^{-1} are typical: however, to cater for variations in speed of response, the slowest listener governs the speed at which data transfer takes place.

Typical IEEE-488 bus configuration

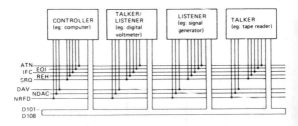

IEEE-488 software

In order to make use of an IEEE-488 bus interface, it is necessary to have a DOS resident driver to simplify the task of interfacing with control software. The requisite driver is invariably supplied with the interface hardware (ie, the IEEE-488 expansion card). The driver is installed as part of the normal system initialisation and configuration routine and, thereafter, will provide a software interface to applications packages or bespoke software written in a variety of languages (eg, BASIC, Pascal, and C). The user and/or programmer is then able to access the facilities offered by the

IEEE-488 bus using high-level IEEE-488 commands such as
REMOTE, LOCAL, ENTER, OUTPUT, etc.

The following are a typical set of high-level language commands
which may be used to program an IEEE-488 system:

Command	Function
ABORT	Terminate the current selected device and command. If no device is given, the bus is cleared and set to the state given in the last CONFIG command eg **ABORT 1** terminates device 1
CLEAR	Clear or reset the selected devices or all devices. If no device is given, the bus is cleared and set to the state given in the last CONFIG command eg **CLEAR 10** resets device 10
CONFIG	Configures the bus to a given set of requirements. The bus will remain in the configured state until it is reconfigured eg **CONFIG TALK = 2 LISTEN = 1,3,4** configures device number 2 as a talker and devices 1, 3, and 4 as listeners
ENTER	Enters bus data from the selected device into a specified string array (the array must have been previously dimensioned). A flag (FLAG%) will contain any error codes returned eg **ENTER 10[$, 0, 15]** enters data from address 10, array elements 0 to 18
EOI	Sends a data byte to the selected device with EOI asserted. The bus must have been programmed to talk before the command is executed. The variable contains the data to be transferred eg **EOI 12[$]** issues an EOI with the last byte of the string to listener 12
LOCAL	Sets the selected device(s) to the local state. If no device is specified then all devices on the bus are set to local eg **LOCAL 10, 11** sets devices 10 and 11 to local state
LOCKOUT	Locks out (on a local basis) the specified device(s). The devices cannot be set to local except by the bus controller eg **LOCKOUT 9, 10** performs a local lockout on devices 9 and 10
OUTPUT	Outputs a string to the selected listener(s). If no listener is specified in the command then all listeners will receive the specified string eg **OUTPUT 9, 11 [$E]** outputs the specified string using even parity

Command	*Function*
PARPOL	Reads the status byte for the devices which have been set for parallel polling eg **PARPOL** reads status byte from a parallel polled device
PASCTL	Passes control of the bus to the specified device. Thereafter, the issuing PC controller will adopt the role of talker/listener eg **PASCTL 5** passes control of the bus to device 5 (which must be a bus controller)
PPCONF	Sets the parallel polling configuration for the specified device eg **PPCONF 12** selects parallel polling for device 12
PPUNCF	Resets the parallel polling configuration for the specified device eg **PPUNCF 12** de-selects parallel polling for device 12
REMOTE	Selects remote operation for the specified device(s) eg **REMOTE 9, 10, 11** selects remote operation for devices 9, 10, and 11
REQUEST	Requests service from an active bus controller (used only when the computer itself is the current bus controller) eg **REQUEST** requests service from the current bus controller
STATUS	Reads a (serial polled) status byte from the selected device eg **STATUS 8** reads the status byte (serial polled) from device 8
SYSCON	Configures the system for a particular user configuration. The command initialises a number of system variables including:

	MAD	the address of the system controller
	CIC	the controller board in charge (more than one IEEE-488 bus controller board may be fitted to a computer)
	NOB	the number of IEEE-488 bus controller boards fitted (1 or 2)
	BA0	the base I/O address for the first bus controller board (ie, board 1)
	BA1	the base I/O address for the second bus controller board (ie, board 2)

eg
SYSCON MAD = 3, CIC = 1, NOB = 1, BA0 = &H300
configures the system as follows:
Computer bus controller address = 3
Controller board in charge = 1
Number of boards fitted = 1
Base address of the controller board = 300 hex

Command Function

TIMEOUT   Sets the timeout duration when transferring data to
          and from devices. An integer number (eg, VAR%) in
          the range 0 to 65000 is used to specify the time. For
          a standard IBM-PC/XT the time (in seconds) is
          equivalent to 3.5•VAR% whilst for an IBM-PC/AT the
          time is approximately 1.5•VAR%
TRIGGER   Sends a trigger message to the selected device (or
          group of devices)
          eg
          TRIGGER 9, 10 triggers devices 9 and 10
Note: If a command is issued by a device which is not the
current controller then an error condition will exist.

IEEE-488 programming

Programming an IEEE-488 system is relatively straightforward
and it is often possible to pass all control information to the DOS
resident software driver in the form of an ASCII encoded string.
The command string is typically followed by three further
parameters:

(a) the variable to be used for output or input (either an integer
    number or a string)
(b) a flag (integer number) which contains the status of the data
    transaction (eg, an error or transfer message code)
(c) the address of the interface board (either 0 or 1 or the physical
    I/O base address)

A command is executed by means of a CALL to the relevant DOS
interrupt. The syntax of an interpreted BASIC (BASIC-A or
GWBASIC) statement would thus be:

CALL IEEE(CMD$, VAR$, FLAG%, BRD%)

where:
IEEE   is the DOS interrupt number
CMD$ is the ASCII command string
VAR$ is the variable to be passed (where numeric data is to
         be passed, VAR$ is replaced by VAR%)
FLAG%   is the status or error code, and
BRD%   is the board number (0 or 1)

As an example, the following GWBASIC code configures a system
and then receives data from device 10, printing the value received
on the screen:

```
100    REM System configuration
110    DEF SEG = &H2000
120    BLOAD "GPIBBASI.BIN",0
130    IEEE = 0
140    FLAG% = 0
150    BRD% = &H300
160    CMD$ = "SYSCON MAD = 3, CIC = 1, NOB = 1, BA0 = 768"
170    CALL IEEE(CMD$, A$, FLAG%, BRD%)
```

```
180    PRINT "System configuration status: ";HEX$(FLAG%)
200    REM Get string data from device 10
210    B$ = SPACE$(18)
220    CMD$ = "REMOTE 10"
230    CALL IEEE(CMD$, B$, FLAG%, BRD%)
240    PRINT "Remote device 10 return flag: ";HEX$(FLAG%)
250    CMD$ = "ENTER 10[$, 0, 17]"
260    CALL IEEE(CMD$, B$, FLAG%, BRD%)
270    PRINT "Enter from device 10 return flag: ";
       HEX$(FLAG%)
280    PRINT "Data received from device 10:         ";B$
290    END
```

Line 110 defines the start address of a block of RAM into which
the low-level interrupt code is loaded from the binary file
GPIBBASI.BIN (line 120). The IEEE interrupt number (0) is
allocated in line 130 whilst the message/status code is
initialised in line 140. Line 150 selects the base I/O address (in
this example, for the Metrabyte MBC-488 board) and the system
configuration command string is defined in line 160 (note that
the PC bus controller is given address 3 and a single IEEE-488
bus interface board is present).

The status flag (returned after configuring the system by
means of the CALL made in line 170) is displayed on the screen
in hexadecimal format (line 180). An empty string (B$) is
initialised in line 210 (this will later receive the data return from
device 10). Device 10 is selected as the remote device in lines
220 and 230 whilst line 240 prints the returned status flag for
this operation. Data is then read from device 10 (lines 250 and
260) and, finally, the status code and returned data are
displayed in lines 270 and 280.

In most cases, it will not be necessary to display returned
status codes. However, it is usually necessary to check these
codes in order to ascertain whether a particular bus transaction
has been successful and that no errors have occurred.
Furthermore, a more modern BASIC (eg, Microsoft QuickBASIC)
will allow programmers to develop a more structured approach
to controlling the IEEE-488 interface with command definitions,
error checks, and CALLs consigned to sub-programs.

Serial I/O devices

Since the data present on a microprocessor bus exists primarily in
parallel form (it is *byte wide*) serial I/O is somewhat more complex
than parallel I/O. Serial input requires a means of conversion of the
serial input data to parallel data in a form which can be presented
to the bus. Conversely, serial output requires a means of conversion
of the parallel data present on the bus into serial output data. In
the first case, conversion can be performed with a serial input
parallel output (SIPO) shift register whilst in the second case a
parallel input serial output (PISO) shift register is required.

Serial data may be transferred in either *synchronous* or
asynchronous mode. In the former case, all transfers are carried out
in accordance with a common clock signal (the clock must be

available at both ends of the transmission path). Asynchronous operation involves transmission of data in *packets*; each packet containing the necessary information required to decode the data which it contains. Clearly this technique is more complex but it has the considerable advantage that a separate clock signal is not required. As with programmable parallel I/O devices, a variety of different names are used to describe programmable serial I/O devices but the *asynchronous communications interface adaptor* (ACIA) and *universal asynchronous receiver/transmitter* (UART) are both commonly encountered in data communications.

Signal connections commonly used with serial I/O devices include:

Signal	Function
D0 to D7	Data input/output lines connected directly to the microprocessor bus
RXD	Received data (incoming serial data)
TXD	Transmitted data (outgoing serial data)
CTS	Clear to send. This (invariably active low) signal is taken low by the peripheral when it is ready to accept data from the microprocessor system
RTS	Request to send. This (invariably active low) signal is taken low by the microprocessor system when it is about to send data to the peripheral.

As with parallel I/O, signals from serial I/O devices are invariably TTL-compatible. It should be noted that, in general, such signals are unsuitable for anything other than the shortest of transmission paths (eg, between a keyboard and a computer system enclosure). Serial data transmission over any appreciable distance invariably requires additional *line drivers* to provide buffering and level shifting between the serial I/O device and the physical medium. Additionally, *line receivers* are required to condition and modify the incoming signal to TTL levels.

Parallel to serial data conversion

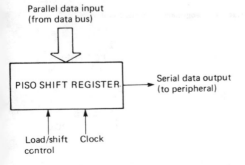

Serial to parallel data conversion

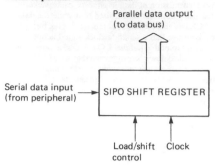

Internal architecture of a representative serial I/O device

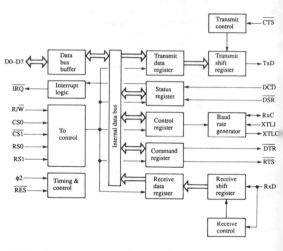

CPU interface to a programmable serial I/O device

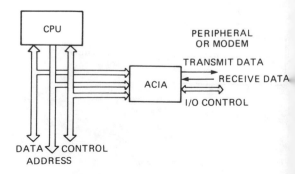

Popular VLSI support devices

Parallel I/O devices

6520	Peripheral interface adaptor (PIA)
6521	Peripheral interface adaptor (PIA) – similar to the 6520
6522	Versatile interface adaptor (VIA)
6820	Peripheral interface adaptor (PIA) – equivalent to the 6520
6821	Peripheral interface adaptor (PIA) – equivalent to the 6521
8255	Programmable parallel interface (PPI)
Z80-PIO	Programmable input/output (PIO)

IEEE-488 bus controllers

68488	General-purpose bus interface adapter
8291A	General-purpose interface bus talker/listener
8292	General-purpose interface bus controller

General purpose serial I/O devices

6850	Asynchronous communications interface adaptor (ACIA)
6852	Synchronous serial data adaptor (SSDA)
8250	Asynchronous communications element
8251	Universal synchronous/asynchronous receiver/transmitter (USART)
8256	Universal asynchronous receiver/transmitter (UART)
Z80-DART	Dual asynchronous receiver/transmitter (DART)
Z80-SIO	Serial input/output controller (SIO)

Communications and enchanced serial I/O devices

16C450	Asynchronous communications element (ACE)
16C452	Dual asynchronous communications element (ACE)
2123	Dual enhanced universal communications element (DEUCE) – based on 8251 but incorporating a baud rate generator
2661	Enhanced programmable communications interface (EPCI)
6551	Asynchronous communications interface adapter (ACIA)
65C51	Asynchronous communications interface adapter (ACIA)
65C52	Dual asynchronous communications interface adapter (DACIA)
68C52	Dual asynchronous communications interface adapter (DACIA)
6854	Advanced data-link controller
68681	Dual universal asynchronous receiver/transmitter (UART)
82C50	Asynchronous communications element (ACE)
8256	Multi-function universal asynchronous receiver/transmitter (MUART)
84C40	Serial input/output controller (SIO)
85C30	Serial communications controller (SCC)
85C35	Serial communications controller (SCC)

| 9902 | Asynchronous communications controller |
| Z8530 | Serial communications controller |

HDLC/SDLC or BSC communications controllers

1935	Synchronous data line controller
65560	Multi-protocol communications controller (MPCC)
68560	Multi-protocol communications controller (MPCC)
68561	Multi-protocol communications controller (MPCC)
82530	Serial communications controller (SCC)
8273	Programmable HDLC/SDLC protocol controller
8274	Multi-protocol serial controller (MPSC)

Network controllers and support devices

68802	Local network controller (LNET)
82586	LAN coprocessor
82588	Single-chip LAN controller
82501	Ethernet serial interface
82C502	Ethernet transceiver

Modem devices and modem controllers

14412	Modem device
7C212A	300/1200 baud modem
7C213	Modem controller
7C214	Modem interface controller
7910	Modem device

Pin connection data for popular programmable parallel I/O devices

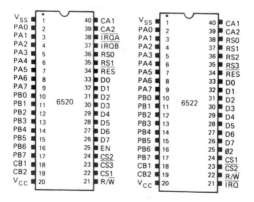

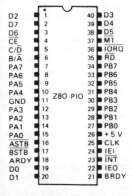

Centronics printer interface

The Centronics interface has established itself as the standard for
parallel data transfer between a microcomputer and a printer. The
standard is based on 36-way Amphenol connector (part no: 57–
30360) and is suitable for distances of up to 2 m.

Parallel data is tranferred into the printer's internal buffer when a
strobe pulse is sent. Handshaking is accomplished by means of
acknowledge (ACKNLG) and busy (BUSY) signals.

Centronics printer interface pin assignment

Pin No.	Abbreviation	Signal/function
1	STROBE	Strobe (active low to read data)
2	DATA 1	Data line 1

Pin No.	Abbreviation	Signal/function
3	DATA 2	Data line 2
4	DATA 3	Data line 3
5	DATA 4	Data line 4
6	DATA 5	Data line 5
7	DATA 6	Data line 6
8	DATA 7	Data line 7
9	DATA 8	Data line 8
10	ACKNLG	Acknowledge (pulsed low to indicate that data has been received)
11	BUSY	Busy (taken high under the following conditions: (a) during data entry (b) during a printing operation (c) when the printer is OFF-LINE (d) during print error status)
12	PE	Paper end (taken high to indicate that the printer is out of paper)
13	SLCT	Select (taken high to indicate that the printer is in the selected state)
14	AUTO FEED XT	Automatic feed (when this input is taken low, the printer is instructed to produce an automatic line feed after printing. This function can be selected internally by means of a DIP switch)
15	n.c.	Not connected (unused)
16	0V	Logic ground
17	CHASSIS GND	Printer chassis (normally isolated from logic ground at the printer)
18	n.c.	Not connected (unused)
19 to 30	GND	Signal ground (originally defined as 'twisted pair earth returns' for pin numbers 1 to 12 inclusive)
31	INIT	Initialize (this line is pulsed low to reset the printer controller)
32	ERROR	Error (taken low by the printer to indicate: (a) PAPER END state (b) OFF-LINE state (c) error state)
33	GND	Signal ground
34	n.c.	Not connected (unused)
35	LOGIC 1	Logic 1 (usually pulled high via 3.3.kohm)
36	SLCT IN	Select input (data entry to the printer is only possible when this line is taken low, but this function may be disabled by means of an internal DIP switch)

Notes:
(a) Signals, pin numbers, and signal directions apply to the printer.
(b) Alternative types of connecter (such as 25-way D type, PCB edge, etc.) are commonly used at the microcomputer.
(c) All signals are standard TTL levels.
(d) ERROR and ACKNLG signals are not supported on some interfaces.

Centronics interface pin connections

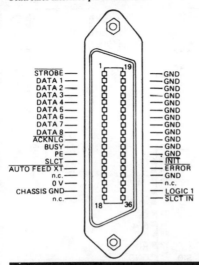

Serial data transmission

In serial data transmission one data bit is transmitted after another. In order to transmit a byte of data it is therefore necessary to convert incoming parallel data from the bus into a serial bit stream which can be transmitted along a line.

Serial data transmission can be synchronous (clocked) or asynchronous (non-clocked). The latter method has obvious advantages and is by far the most popular method. The rate at which data is transmitted is given by the number of bits transmitted per unit time. The commonly adopted unit is the 'baud', with 1 baud roughly equivalent to 1 bit per second.

It should, however, be noted that there is a subtle difference between the bit rate as perceived by the computer and the baud rate present in the transmission medium. The reason is simply that some overhead in terms of additional synchronizing bits is required in order to recover asynchronously transmitted data.

In the case of a typical RS-232C link, a total of 11 bits is required to transmit only seven bits of data. A line baud rate of 600 baud thus represents a useful data transfer rate of only some 382 bits per second.

Many modern serial data transmission systems can trace their origins to the 20 mA current loop interface which was once commonly used to connect a teletype unit to the minicomputer system. This system was based on the following logic levels:

Mark = logic 1 = 20mA current flowing

Space = logic 0 = no current flowing

where the terms 'mark' and 'space' simply refer to the presence or absence of a current.

This system was extended to cater for more modern and more complex peripherals for which voltage, rather than current, levels were appropriate.

Pin connection data for popular programmable serial I/O devices

8251

Pin	Signal		Pin	Signal
1	D2		28	D1
2	D3		27	D0
3	RXD		26	V_{CC}
4	GND		25	$\overline{RXC}$
5	D4		24	$\overline{DTR}$
6	D5		23	$\overline{RTS}$
7	D6		22	$\overline{DSR}$
8	D7		21	RESET
9	$\overline{TXC}$		20	CLK
10	$\overline{WR}$		19	TXD
11	$\overline{CS}$		18	TXEMPTY
12	$C/\overline{D}$		17	CTS
13	$\overline{RD}$		16	SYNDET
14	RXRDY		15	TXRDY

6850

Pin	Signal		Pin	Signal
1	V_{SS}		24	$\overline{CTS}$
2	RXD		23	$\overline{DCD}$
3	RXCLK		22	D0
4	TXCLK		21	D1
5	RTS		20	D2
6	TXD		19	D3
7	$\overline{IR}$		18	D4
8	CS0		17	D5
9	CS2		16	D6
10	CS1		15	D7
11	RS		14	EN
12	V_{dd}		13	$R/\overline{W}$

Z80-SIO

Pin	Signal		Pin	Signal
1	D1		40	D0
2	D3		39	D2
3	D5		38	D4
4	$\overline{D7}$		37	D6
5	$\overline{INT}$		36	$\overline{IORQ}$
6	IEI		35	$\overline{CE}$
7	$\overline{IEO}$		34	$B/\overline{A}$
8	M1		33	$C/\overline{D}$
9	V_{CC}		32	$\overline{RD}$
10	$\overline{W/RDYA}$		31	GND
11	SYNCA		30	$\overline{W/RDYB}$
12	RXDA		29	$\overline{RXDB}$
13	$\overline{RXCA}$		28	RXCB
14	$\overline{TXCA}$		27	TXCB
15	TXDA		26	TXDB
16	$\overline{DTRA}$		25	$\overline{DTRB}$
17	$\overline{RTSA}$		24	$\overline{RTSB}$
18	$\overline{CTSA}$		23	$\overline{CTSB}$
19	$\overline{DCDA}$		22	$\overline{DCDB}$
20	CLK		21	RESET

6402

Pin	Signal		Pin	Signal
1	V_{CC}		40	TRC
2	NC		39	EPE
3	GND		38	CLS 1
4	$\overline{RRD}$		37	CLS 2
5	$\overline{RBR8}$		36	SBS
6	RBR7		35	PI
7	RBR6		34	CRL
8	$\overline{RBR5}$		33	TBR8
9	$\overline{RBR4}$		32	TBR7
10	RBR3		31	TBR6
11	RBR2		30	TBR5
12	RBR1		29	TBR4
13	PE		28	TBR3
14	$\overline{FE}$		27	TBR2
15	$\overline{OE}$		26	TBR1
16	SFD		25	TRO
17	RRC		24	$\overline{TRE}$
18	$\overline{DRR}$		23	$\overline{TBRL}$
19	$\overline{DR}$		22	TBRE
20	RRI		21	MR

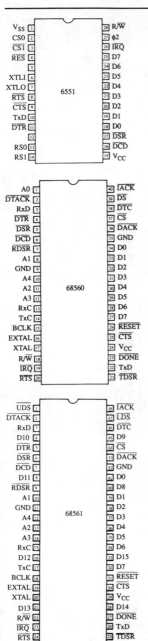

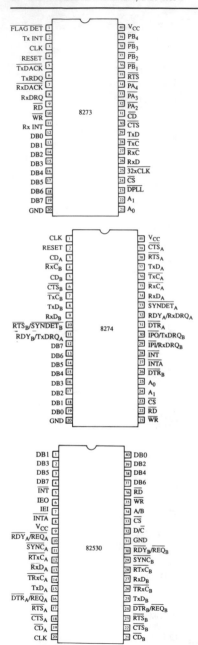

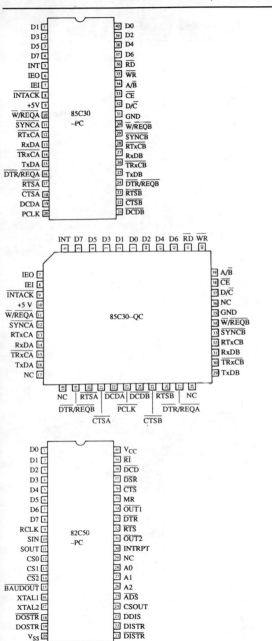

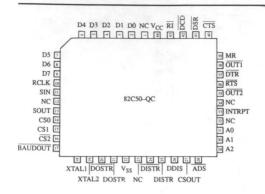

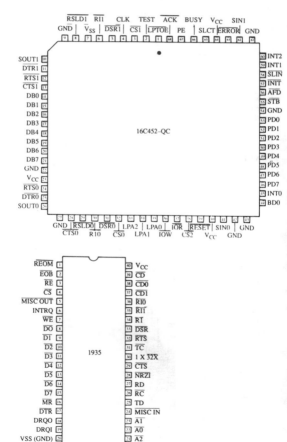

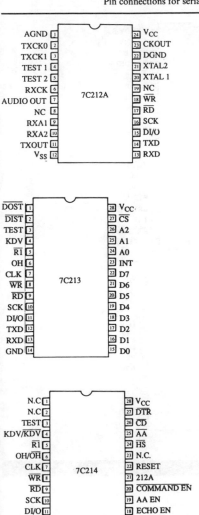

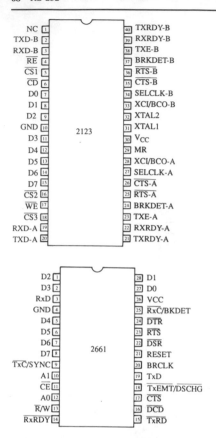

RS-232

The RS-232/CCITT V.24 interface undoubtedly reigns supreme as the most widely used standard for serial communication between microcomputers, peripheral devices, and remote host computers. The RS-232D EIA standard (January 1987) is a revision of the earlier RS-232C standard which brings it in-line with international standards CCITT V.24, V.28 and ISO IS2110. The RS-232D standard includes facilities for loop-back testing which were not defined under RS-232C.

RS-232 was first defined by the Electronic Industries Association (EIA) in 1962 as a recommended standard (RS) for modem interfacing. The standard relates essentially to two types of equipment; *data terminal equipment* (DTE) and *data circuit-terminating equipment* (DCE).

Data terminal equipment (eg a microcomputer) is capable of sending and/or receiving data via an RS-232 serial interface. It is thus said to terminate a serial link. Data circuit terminating equipment (formerly known as *data communications equipment*), on the other hand, is generally thought of as a device which can facilitate serial data communications and a typical example is that of a modem (modulator-demodulator) which forms an essential link in the serial path between a microcomputer and a conventional analogue telephone line.

An RS-232 serial port is usually implemented using a standard 25-way D-connector. Data terminal equipment is normally fitted with a male connector while data circuit-terminating equipment conventionally uses a female connector (note that there are some exceptions to this rule!).

RS-232 signals

RS-232 signals fall into one of the following three categories:

(a) data (eg, TXD, RXD)

RS-232 provides for two independent serial data channels (described as *primary* and *secondary*). Both of these channels provide for full duplex operation (ie, simultaneous transmission and reception).

(b) handshake control (eg, RTS, CTS)

Handshake signals provide the means by which the flow of serial data is controlled allowing, for example, a DTE to open a dialogue with the DCE prior to actually transmitting data over the serial data path.

(c) timing (eg, TC, RC)

For synchronous (rather than the more usual asynchronous) mode of operation, it is necessary to pass clock signals between the devices. These timing signals provide a means of synchronising the received signal to allow successful decoding.

The complete set of RS-232D signals is summarised in the following table, together with EIA and CCITT designations and commonly used signal line abbreviations.

RS-232D signals and functions

Pin Number	EIA interchange circuit	CCITT equiv.	Common abbreviations	Direction	Signal/function
1	—	—	FG	—	frame or protective ground
2	BA	103	TD or TXD	To DCE	transmitted data
3	BB	104	RD or RXD	To DTE	received data
4	CA	105	RTS	To DCE	request to send
5	CB	106	CTS	To DTE	clear to send
6	CC	107	DSR	To DTE	DCE ready
7	AB	102	SG	—	signal ground/ common return
8	CF	109	DCD	To DTE	received line

Pin Number	EIA interchange circuit	Common abbreviations	Direction	Signal/function
				signal detector
9	—	—	—	reserved for testing (positive test voltage)
10	—	—	—	reserved for testing (negative test voltage)
11	—	[QM]	—	[Equaliser mode]
12	SCF/ CI	122/ 112	SDCD	secondary received line signal detector/ data rate select (DCE source)
13	SCB	121	SCTS	To DTE	secondary clear to send
14	SBA	118	STD	To DCE	secondary transmitted data
15	DB	114	TC	To DTE	transmit signal element timing (DCE source)
16	SBB	119	SRD	To DTE	secondary received data
17	DD	115	RC	To DTE	receiver signal element timing (DCE source)
18	LL	141	[DCR]	To DCE	local loop-back [Divided receive clock]
19	SCA	120	SRTS	To DCE	secondary request to send
20	CD	108.2	DTR	To DCE	data terminal ready
21	RL/ CG	140/ 110	SQ	To DCE/ To DTE	remote loop-back/ signal quality detector
22	CE	125	RI	To DTE	ring indicator
23	CH/ CI	111/ 112	—	To DCE/ To DTE	data signal rate selector (DTE)/ data signal rate selector (DCE)
24	DA	113	TC	To DCE	transmit signal element timing [DTE source]
25	TM	142	—	To DTE	test mode

Notes:

1. The functions given in brackets for lines 11 and 18 relate to the Bell 113B and 208A specifications
2. Lines 9 and 10 are normally reserved for testing. A typical use for these lines is testing of the positive and negative voltage levels used to represent the MARK and SPACE levels
3. For new designs using EIA interchange circuit SCF, CH and CI

are assigned to pin-23. If SCF is not used, CI is assigned to pin-12

4. Some manufacturers use spare RS-232 lines for testing and/or special functions peculiar to particular hardware (some equipment even feeds power and analogue signals along unused RS-232C lines!)

In practice, few RS-232 implementations make use of the secondary channel and, since asynchronous (non-clocked) operation is the norm, only eight or nine of the 25 are regularly used.

Subset of the most commonly used RS-232 signals

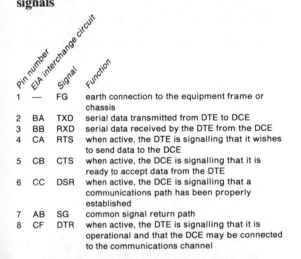

Pin number	EIA interchange circuit	Signal	Function
1	—	FG	earth connection to the equipment frame or chassis
2	BA	TXD	serial data transmitted from DTE to DCE
3	BB	RXD	serial data received by the DTE from the DCE
4	CA	RTS	when active, the DTE is signalling that it wishes to send data to the DCE
5	CB	CTS	when active, the DCE is signalling that it is ready to accept data from the DTE
6	CC	DSR	when active, the DCE is signalling that a communications path has been properly established
7	AB	SG	common signal return path
8	CF	DTR	when active, the DTE is signalling that it is operational and that the DCE may be connected to the communications channel

RS-232 waveforms

In most RS-232 systems, data is transmitted asynchronously as a series of packets, each representing a single ASCII character and containing sufficient information for it to be decoded without the need for a separate clock signal.

ASCII characters are represented by seven binary digits (bits). The upper case letter *A*, for example, is represented by the seven-bit binary word; 1000001. In order to send the letter *A* via an RS-232 system, we need to add extra bits to signal the start and end of the data packet. These are known as the *start bit* and *stop bit* respectively. In addition, we may wish to include a further bit to provide a simple parity error detecting facility.

One of the most commonly used schemes involves the use of one start bit, one parity bit, and two stop bits. The commencement of the data packet is signalled by the start bit which is always low

irrespective of the contents of the packet. The start bit is followed
by the seven data bits representing the ASCII character concerned.
A parity bit is added to make the resulting number of 1s in the
group either odd (*odd parity*) or even (*even parity*). Finally, two
stop bits are added. These are both high.

The complete asynchronously transmitted data word thus
comprises eleven bits (note that only seven of these actually contain
data). In binary terms the word can be represented as:
01000001011. In this case, even parity has been used and thus the
ninth (*parity bit*) is a 0.

Voltage levels employed in an RS-232 interface are markedly
different from those used within a microcomputer system. A
positive voltage (of between + 3 V and + 25 V) is used to represent
a logic 0 (or *space*) while a negative voltage (of between − 3 V and
− 25 V) is used to represent a logic 1 (or *mark*).

Level shifting (from TTL to RS-232 signal levels and vice versa)
is invariably accomplished using *line driver* and *line receiver* chips,
the most common examples being the 1488 and 1489 devices.

**Typical representation of the ASCII character *A* using TTL signal
levels**

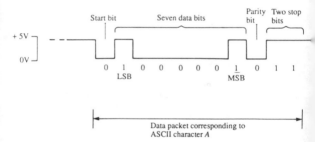

ASCII character *A* as it appears on TD or RD signal lines

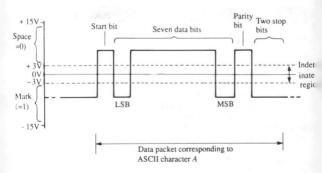

RS-232 electrical characteristics

The following summarises the principal electrical specification for the RS-232 standard:

Maximum line driver output voltage (open circuit): ±25 V
Maximum line driver output current (short circuit): ±500 mA
Minimum line impedance: 3 kΩ in parallel with 2.5 nF
Line driver space output voltage ($3 \text{ k}\Omega \leq R_L \leq 7 \text{ k}\Omega$):
+5 V to +15 V
Line driver mark output voltage ($3 \text{ k}\Omega \leq R_L \leq 7 \text{ k}\Omega$):
−5 V to −15 V
Line driver output (idle state): mark
Line receiver output with open circuit input: logic 1
Line receiver output with input ≥ 3 V: logic 0
Line receiver output with input ≥ -3 V: logic 1

Maximum transition times are defined as follows:

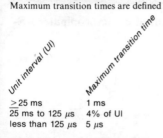

Unit interval (UI)	Maximum transition time
≥ 25 ms	1 ms
25 ms to 125 μs	4% of UI
less than 125 μs	5 μs

RS-232 logic and voltage levels

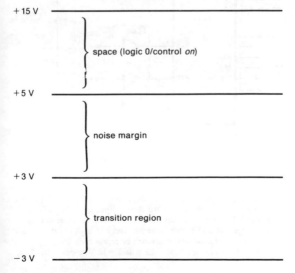

+ 15 V

space (logic 0/control *on*)

+ 5 V

noise margin

+ 3 V

transition region

− 3 V

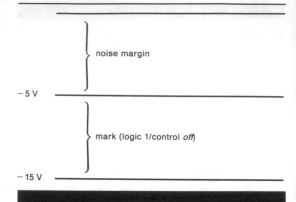

Simplified arrangement of a microcomputer RS-232 interface

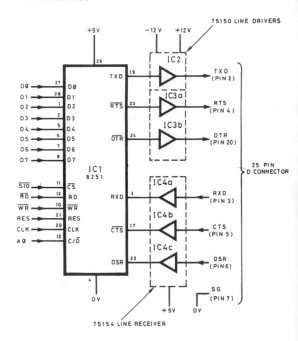

IC1 is a programmable serial I/O device whilst IC2 and IC3 provide level shifting and buffering for the three output signals (TXD, RTS and DTR). IC4 provides level shifting for the three input signals (RXD, CTS and DSR). Note that IC2 and IC3 both require ± 12 V supplies and that mark and space will be represented by approximate voltage levels of − 12 V and + 12 V respectively.

RS-232 enhancements

Several further standards have been introduced in order to overcome some of the shortcomings of the original RS-232 specification. These generally provide for better line matching, increased distance capability, and faster data rates. Notable among these systems are RS-422 (a balanced system which caters for a line impedance as low as 50 ohm), RS-423 (an unbalanced system which will tolerate a line impedance of 450 ohm minimum), and RS-449 (a very fast serial data standard which uses a number of changed circuit functions and a 37-way D connector).

RS-422

RS-422 is a balanced system (differential signal lines are used) which employs lower line voltage levels than those employed with RS-232. Space is represented by a line voltage level in the range $+2$ V to $+6$ V while mark is represented by a line voltage level in the range -2 V to -6 V. RS-422 caters for a line impedance of as low as 50 ohm and supports data rates of up to 10 Mbps.

RS-422 logic and voltage levels

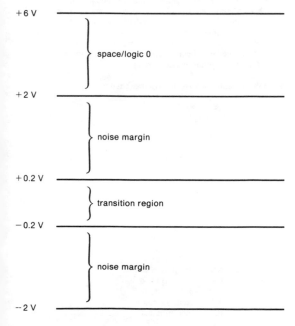

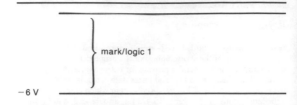

RS-423

Unlike RS-422, RS-423 employs an unbalanced line configuration (a single signal line is used in conjunction with signal ground). Line voltage levels of +4 V to +6 V and −4 V to −6 V represent space and mark respectively and the standard specifies a minimum line terminating resistance of 450 ohm. RS-423 supports a maximum data rate of 100 kbps.

RS-449

RS-449 is a further enhancement of RS-422 and RS-423 which caters for very fast data rates (up to 2 Mbps) yet provides for upward compatability with RS-232. Ten extra circuit functions have been provided while three of the original interchange circuits have been abandoned. In order to minimise confusion, and since certain changes have been made to the definition of circuit functions, a completely new set of circuit abbreviations has been developed. In addition, the standard requires 37-way and 9-way D-connectors, the latter being necessary where use is made of the secondary channel interchange circuits.

RS-449 pin connection and interchange circuits

Auxiliary connector (9-way)	Main connector (37-way) A	B	Circuit abbreviation	Function
1	1			shield
5	19		SG	signal ground
9	37		SC	send common
6	20		RC	receive common
	4	22	SD	send data
	6	24	RD	receive data
	7	25	RS	request to send
	9	27	CS	clear to send
	11	29	DM	data mode
	12	30	TR	terminal ready
	15		IC	incoming call

Auxiliary connector (9-way) A	Main connector (37-way) B	Circuit abbreviation	Function
13	31	RR	receive ready
33		SQ	signal quality
16		SR	signalling rate selector
2		SI	signalling rate indicator
17	35	TT	terminal timing
5	23	ST	send timing
8	26	RT	receive timing
	3	SSD	secondary send data
	4	SRD	secondary receive data
	7	SRS	secondary request to send
	8	SCS	secondary clear to send
	2	SRR	secondary receiver ready
10		LL	local loop-back
14		RL	remote loop-back
18		TM	test mode
32		SS	select standby
36		SB	standby indicator
18		SF	select frequency
28		IS	terminal in service
34		NS	new signal

Notes:
1. Pins 3 and 31 of the 37-way connector are undefined
2. B on the main connector indicates a return signal

RS-423 logic and voltage levels

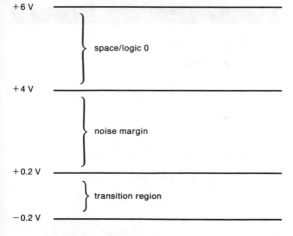

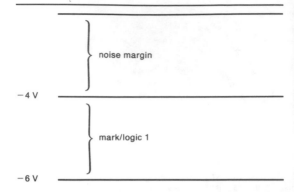

noise margin

−4 V

mark/logic 1

−6 V

Electrical characteristics of popular interface specifications

Interface specification	Mode	Line	Voltage levels		Logic levels		Data rate (maximum)
			min	max	0	1	bps
V24/V28	asynchronous/ synchronous	unbalanced	3 V	25 V	+ve	−ve	19.2 K
RS-232C	asynchronous/ synchronous	unbalanced	3 V	25 V	+ve	−ve	19.2 K
X26 (V10)	asynchronous/ synchronous	unbalanced	3 V	10 V	+ve	−ve	100 K
RS-423A	asynchronous/ synchronous	unbalanced	0.2 V	6 V	+ve	−ve	100 K
X27 (V11)	asynchronous/ synchronous	balanced	0.3 V	10 V	+ve	−ve	10 M
RS-422A	asynchronous/ synchronous	balanced	0.2 V	6 V	+ve	−ve	10 M

RS-232 data cables

(a) 4-way cable for dumb terminals

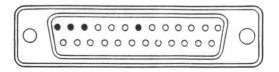

Pins used: 1–3 and 7 (pins 8 and 20 are jumpered)

(b) 9-way cable for asynchronous communications

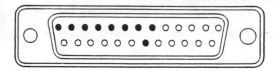

Pins used: 1–8 and 20

(c) 15-way cable for synchronous communications

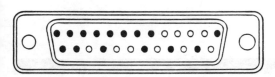

Pins used: 1–8, 13, 15, 17, 20, 22 and 24

(d) 25-way cable for universal applications

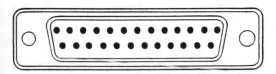

Pins used: 1–25

Male and female 25-way D-connectors used for RS-232

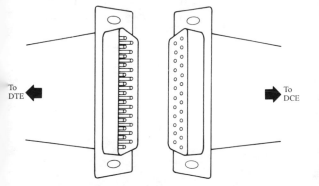

RS-232 pin connections

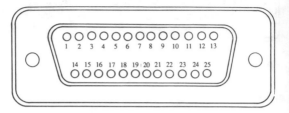

(Pin view of connector)

RS-449 pin connections

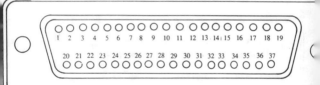

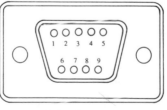

(Pin view of connectors)

RS-232 signals and pin connections

Left side		Right side
Secondary transmitted data, STD	14	Frame ground (1)
Transmit signal element timing, TC (DCE source)	15	Transmitted data, TD (2)
Secondary received data, SRD	16	Received data, RD (3)
Receive signal element timing, RC	17	Request to send, RTS (4)
Local loop-back, LL	18	Clear to send, CTS (5)
Secondary request to send, SRTS	19	DCE ready, DSR (6)
Data terminal ready, DTR	20	Signal ground (7)
Remote loop-back, RL	21	Received line signal detector, DCD (8)
Ring indicator, RI	22	Reserved for testing (9)
Data signal rate selector	23	Reserved for testing (10)
Transmit signal element timing, TC (DTE source)	24	Unassigned (11)
Test mode	25	Secondary received line signal detector/data rate select, SDCD (12)
		Secondary clear to send, SCTS (13)

S5/8 interface standard

The RS-232 and V.24 standards are unnecessarily complex for many applications and a simpler serial interface using conventional TTL voltage levels has much to recommend for less critical applications. A minimal but nevertheless elegant solution is provided by the new S5/8 standard. This standard (currently awaiting BS approval) uses nominal 5 V levels in conjunction with an 8-pin DIN connector.

The S5/8 standard specifies two classes of device. A D-device incorporates its own power supply and can provide power (+ 5 V at up to 20 mA) at the S5/8 connector. An S-device, on the other hand, does not have a supply of its own but may derive its power from an associated D-device. A typical example of an S-device connected to a D-device would be a modem connected to a personal microcomputer. Although there is an obvious difference between D and S-devices as regards power supplies, they are considered to be on an equal footing as far as data transfers are concerned.

The pin assignment of the standard 8-way DIN connector used by S5/8 is as follows:

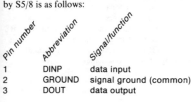

Pin number	Abbreviation	Signal/function
1	DINP	data input
2	GROUND	signal ground (common)
3	DOUT	data output

Pin number	Abbreviation	Signal/function
4	HINP	handshake input
5	HOUT	handshake output
6	SINP	secondary input
7	SOUT	secondary output
8	V+	+5 V (20 mA maximum)
Screen	EARTH	earthed screen

This arrangement ensures that input and output signals are paired in opposite sides of the connector (as in audio practice). It should also be noted that a standard 180 degree 5-pin DIN plug will mate with the 8-pin DIN connector specified in S5/8. This arrangement will give access to all signals with the exception of the secondary communication circuits (SINP and SOUT) and +5 V (V+).

The electrical characteristics of the S5/8 interface are as follows:

Inputs

Input resistance:	47 kΩ
Input low threshold:	+0.9 V maximum
Input high threshold:	+3.85 V minimum
Input protection:	±25 V maximum

Outputs

Output low voltage:	+0.15 V maximum
Output high voltage:	+4.35 V minimum
Capacitive load drive capability	2.5 nF minimum
Short-circuit protection:	to any other signal on the interface

S5/8 uses a conventional serial data structure and, in the same sense as RS-232, the line rests low (0 V) and goes high for the start bit. Thereafter, transmitted data bits are inverted. Each frame (serially transmitted data word) comprises one start bit, eight data bits, and one stop bit (ie, 10 bits total). There is no parity bit and hence error detection should be organised on a block-by-block basis using checksum or CRC techniques.

S5/8 specifies a data transfer rate of 9.6 kbps (the fastest of the bit rates widely used with RS-232) and simple handshaking is supported using the HINP and HOUT lines.

Undoubtedly the most attractive feature of S5/8 is that an interface can very easily be realized using nothing more than a UART and a high-speed CMOS inverting buffer (eg, 74HC14). There is no need for line drivers and level shifters that would be essential in order to implement a full-specification RS-232 interface.

Finally, while an S5/8 interface will safely and correctly receive RS-232 signal levels, the reverse is not necessarily true. However, depending upon the level of support for the S5/8 standard, it is expected that a number of manufacturers of low-cost personal computers will adopt an intermediate position by implementing RS-232 ports using 8-way DIN connectors and changing line receivers for high-speed CMOS Schmitt inverters. Such an arrangement will readily permit interworking of the two schemes.

Line drivers and line receivers

Device	Package	EIA standard	Function
1488	14-pin dil	RS-232	quad line driver
14C88	14-pin dil	RS-232	quad line driver (low power)
1489	14-pin dil	RS-232	quad line receiver
14C89	14-pin dil	RS-232	quad line receiver (low power)
26LS31	16-pin dil	RS-422	quad differential line driver
26LS32	16-pin dil	RS-422/RS-423	quad differential line receiver
3486	16-pin dil	RS-422/RS423	quad line receiver
3487	16-pin dil	RS-422	quad line driver
75154	16-pin dil	RS-232	quad line receiver
75155	8-pin dil	RS-232	line driver and line receiver
75172	16-pin dil	RS-422/RS-485	quad differential line driver
75173	16-pin dil	RS-422/RS-423/RS-485	quad differential line receiver
75174	16-pin dil	RS-422/RS-485	quad differential line driver
75175	16-pin dil	RS-422/RS-423/RS-485	quad differential line receiver
75176	8-pin dil	RS-422/RS-485	differential bus transceiver
75177	8-pin dil	RS-422/RS-485	differential bus repeater
75178	8-pin dil	RS-422/RS-485	differential bus repeater
8833	16-pin dil		quad bus transceiver

Line driver and line receiver pin connections

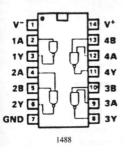

1488

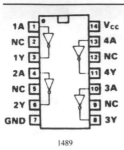

1489

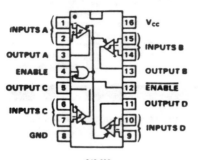

26L531

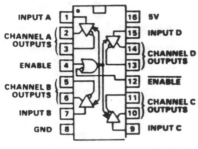

26L532

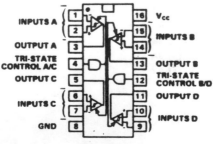

3486

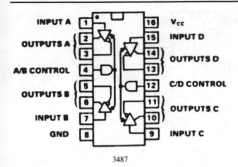

3487

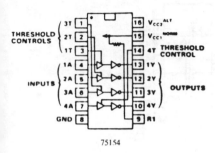

75154

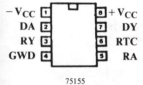

75155

1A [1] Vcc
1Y [2] 4A
1Z [3] 4Y
ENABLE G [4] 4Z
2Z [5] ENABLE Ḡ
2Y [6] 3Z
2A [7] 3Y
GND [8] 3A

75172

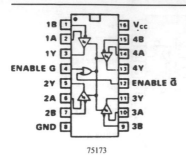

75173

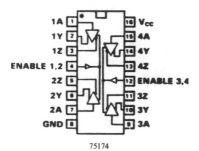

75174

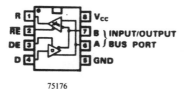

75176

75175

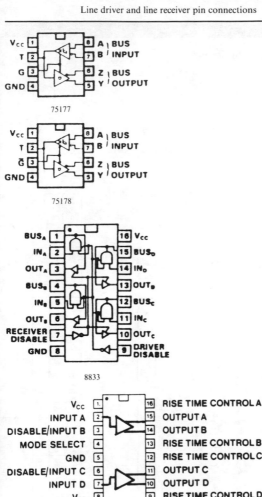

75177

75178

8833

3691

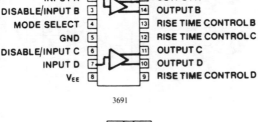

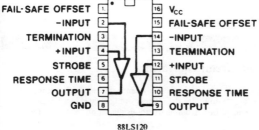

88LS120

Basic logic gates

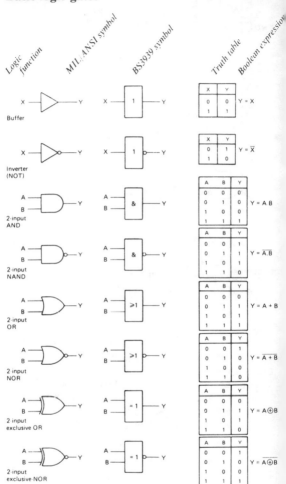

Logic function	MIL/ANSI symbol	BS3939 symbol	Truth table	Boolean expression
Buffer			X Y 0 0 1 1	Y = X
Inverter (NOT)			X Y 0 1 1 0	Y = $\overline{X}$
2-input AND			A B Y 0 0 0 0 1 0 1 0 0 1 1 1	Y = A.B
2-input NAND			A B Y 0 0 1 0 1 1 1 0 1 1 1 0	Y = $\overline{A.B}$
2-input OR			A B Y 0 0 0 0 1 1 1 0 1 1 1 1	Y = A + B
2-input NOR			A B Y 0 0 1 0 1 0 1 0 0 1 1 0	Y = $\overline{A + B}$
2-input exclusive OR			A B Y 0 0 0 0 1 1 1 0 1 1 1 0	Y = A $\oplus$ B
2-input exclusive-NOR			A B Y 0 0 1 0 1 0 1 0 0 1 1 1	Y = $\overline{A \oplus B}$

Logic circuit equivalents

The following logic circuit equivalents are useful when it is
necessary to minimize the number of logic gates in a given
arrangement or when a restriction is placed on the types of gate

available. It should be noted that, while the logical functions will be
identical, the electrical performance may be different. This is
particularly true in the case of propagation delay.

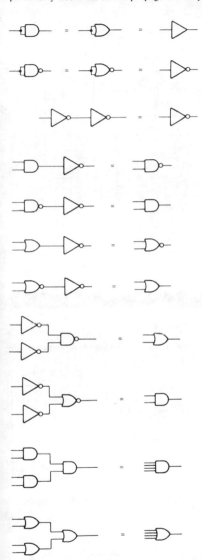

Mixed logic equivalents

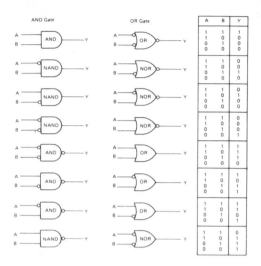

AND Gate	OR Gate	A	B	Y
		1	1	1
		1	0	0
		0	1	0
		0	0	0
		1	1	0
		1	0	0
		0	1	1
		0	0	0
		1	1	0
		1	0	1
		0	1	0
		0	0	0
		1	1	0
		1	0	0
		0	1	0
		0	0	1
		1	1	1
		1	0	1
		0	1	1
		0	0	0
		1	1	1
		1	0	0
		0	1	1
		0	0	1
		1	1	1
		1	0	1
		0	1	0
		0	0	1
		1	1	0
		1	0	1
		0	1	1
		0	0	1

Typical links between computers

Typical link between a microcomputer and a local host computer (both configured as DTE)

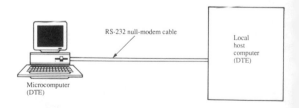

RS-232 null-modem cable

Local host computer (DTE)

Microcomputer (DTE)

Typical link between a microcomputer and a remote host computer (both configured as DTE)

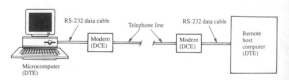

RS-232 data cable Telephone line RS-232 data cable

Modem (DCE) Modem (DCE) Remote host computer (DTE)

Microcomputer (DTE)

Typical link between two microcomputers (both configured as DTE)

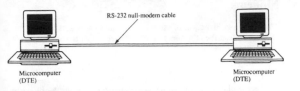

Microcomputer
(DTE)

Microcomputer
(DTE)

Typical null-modem arrangements

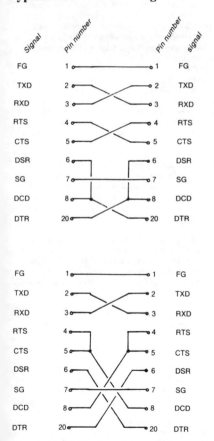

Modems

Modem is a contraction of modulator-demodulator and this
succinctly describes the function of a device which has the dual role
of:

(a) modulating an outgoing baseband signal onto a carrier for
    transmission through a physical medium
(b) demodulating an incoming modulated carrier from the physical
    medium in order to recover an input baseband signal.

The modulation method employed is invariably *frequency shift
keying* (FSK). A space (logic 0) is represented by a sinusoidal signal
of one frequency, while a mark (logic 1) is represented by another.
The frequencies used for the mark and space tones are chosen so
that they can be passed through the transmission medium with
minimal attenuation. Hence, in the case of modems which facilitate
connection via ordinary telephone lines, mark and space must be
represented by audible tones.

The available bandwidth within the transmission medium
(telephone line) also has a bearing upon the signalling rate. A wider
bandwidth will permit signalling (ie, switching between mark and
space tones) at a faster rate. In practice, the maximum signalling
rate for a conventional exchange line is in the region of 1300 baud.
It is, however, possible for a single exchange line to support duplex
working in which case different mark and space frequencies must be
employed for transmit and receive.

Filters are used within modems to separate these frequencies and
each end of the link must employ a different pair of mark and space
frequencies. The frequencies used for setting up a data transfer (ie,
those used for *originate* mode) will thus be different from those
which are used in response to such a request (ie, those used in
answer mode). When communication is established with a larger
remote host, the user-modem will normally establish the call in
originate mode.

Signal frequencies are governed by a number of internationally
agreed standards. Bell standards 103 and 202 are commonly
employed in the United States, while CCITT V.21 and V.23 are
regularly used in Europe. Most modern modems are able to
support a number of standards as well as providing auto-originate/
auto-answer facilities.

Two methods are employed for connection to exchange lines and,
in both cases, electrical isolation between the exchange line and
modem circuitry is an essential requirement. *Acoustic coupling*
involves the use of audible transducers which respectively couple
the transmitted and received signals to the mouthpiece and earpiece
of a conventional telephone handset. This method is a little
cumbersome but is popular with portable modem equipment since
it does not require any direct connection to the line. *Direct connect*
involves transformer coupling to a telephone socket. Transmitted
and received signals are separated using active operational amplifier
techniques.

Communications software is normally required to set up the
serial port to which the modem is connected (via RS-232) and, in
many cases also to configure the modem. Software will generally
provide for a range of signalling speeds (baud rates) and
handshaking protocols (eg, X-ON/X-OFF).

Simplified block schematic of a modem

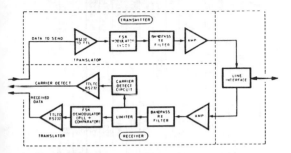

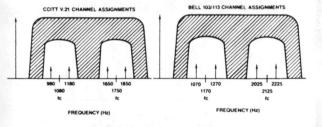

Modem signal frequencies

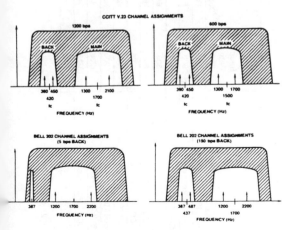

Frequency parameters

Modem	Baud Rate (BPS)	Duplex	Transmit Frequency		Receive Frequency		Answer tone Freq Hz	Soft Turn Off Tone Hz
			Space Hz	Mark Hz	Space Hz	Mark Hz		
Bell 103 Originate	300	Full	1070	1270	2025	2225	—	—
Bell 103 Answer	300	Full	2025	2225	1070	1270	2225	—
CCITT V.21 Originate	300	Full	1180	980	1850	1650	—	—
CCITT V.21 Answer	300	Full	1850	1650	1180	980	2100	—
CCITT V.23 Mode 1	600	Half	1700	1300	1700	1300	2100	900
CCITT V.23 Mode 2	1200	Half	2100	1300	2100	1300	2100	900*
CCITT V.23 Mode 2 Equalized	1200	Half	2100	1300	2100	1300	2100	900*
Bell 202	1200	Half	2200	1200	2200	1200	2025	900
Bell 202 Equalized	1200	Half	2200	1200	2200	1200	2025	900
CCITT V.23 Back	75/150	—	450	390	450	390	—	—
Bell 202 150bps Back	150	—	487	387	487	387	—	—

Note:
*For V.23 soft turn off modes only

V21 frequency spectrum (300/300 baud)

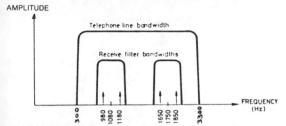

V21 channels for 300/300 baud

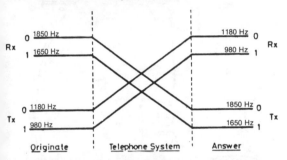

Permitted transmitted spectrum (BS 6305)

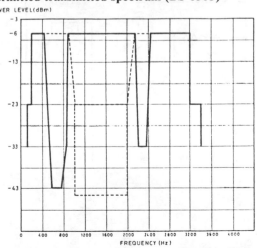

Modem connecting methods

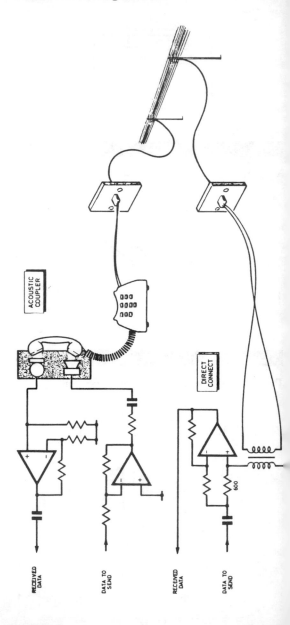

ACOUSTIC COUPLER

DIRECT CONNECT

RECEIVED DATA

DATA TO SEND

RECEIVED DATA

DATA TO SEND

DTMF digits and tone pairs

BCD				Dial digits	Tone pairs	
0	0	0	0	0	941	1336
0	0	0	1	1	697	1209
0	0	1	0	2	697	1336
0	0	1	1	3	697	1477
0	1	0	0	4	770	1209
0	1	0	1	5	770	1336
0	1	1	0	6	770	1477
0	1	1	1	7	852	1209
1	0	0	0	8	852	1336
1	0	0	1	9	852	1477
1	0	1	0	★	941	1209
1	0	1	1	spare (B)	697	1633
1	1	0	0	spare (C)	770	1633
1	1	0	1	spare (D)	852	1633
1	1	1	0	#	941	1477
1	1	1	1	spare (F)	941	1633

Transmitter carrier and signalling frequency specifications

Frequency	Specification (Hz ± 0.01%)
V.22 bis low channel, originate mode	1200
V.22 low channel, originate mode	1200
V.22 high bis channel, answer mode	2400
V.22 high channel, answer mode	2400
Bell 212A high channel, answer mode	2400
Bell 212A low channel, originate mode	1200
Bell 103/113 originating mark	1270
Bell 103/113 originating space	1070
Bell 103/113 answer mark	2225
Bell 103/113 answer space	2025

Line signal encoding (V26A and V26B)

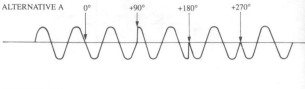

Differential two-phase encoding (V26bis)

1200 bps	
Bit	Phase change
0	+ 90°
1	+ 270°

Differential four-phase encoding (V26A and V26B/Bell 201)

2400 bps		
Dibit	Phase change	
	V.26A	V.26B/Bell 201
00	0°	+ 45°
01	+ 90°	+ 135°
11	+ 180°	+ 225°
10	+ 270°	+ 315°

Typical bit error rate performance for a modem

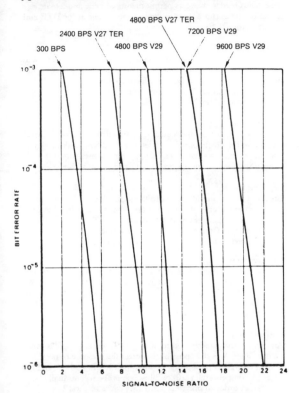

Data communications test equipment

A number of specialised test instruments and accessories are
required for testing data communications systems. The following
items are commonly encountered.

Patch boxes
These low-cost devices facilitate the cross connection of RS-232 (or
equivalent) signal lines. The equipment is usually fitted with two D-
type connectors (or ribbon cables fitted with a plug and socket) and
all lines are brought out to a patching area into which links may be
plugged. In use, these devices are connected in series with the RS-
232 serial data path and various patching combinations are tested
until a functional interface is established. If desired, a dedicated
cable may then be manufactured in order to replace the patch box.

Gender changers

Gender changers normally comprise an extended RS-232 connector which has a male connector at one end and a female connector at the other. Gender changers permit mixing of male and female connector types (note that the convention is male at the DTE and female at the DCE).

Null modems

Like gender changers, these devices are connected in series with an RS-232 serial data path. Their function is simply that of changing the signal lines so that a DTE is effectively configured as a DCE. Null modems can easily be set up using a patch box or manufactured in the form of a dedicated null-modem cable.

Line monitors

Line monitors display the logical state (in terms of mark or space) present on the most commonly used data and handshaking signal lines. Light emitting diodes (LED) provide the user with a rapid indication of which signals are present and active within the system.

Breakout boxes

Breakout boxes provide access to the signal lines and invariably combine the features of patch box and line monitor. In addition, switches or jumpers are usually provided for linking lines on either side of the box. Connection is almost invariably via two 25-way ribbon cables terminated with connectors.

Interface testers

Interface testers are somewhat more complex than simple breakout boxes and generally incorporate facilities for forcing lines into mark or space states, detecting *glitches*, measuring baud rates, and also displaying the format of data words. Such instruments are, not surprisingly, rather expensive.

Oscilloscopes

An oscilloscpe can be used to display waveforms of signals present on data lines. It is thus possible to detect the presence of noise and glitches as well as measuring signal voltage levels, and rise and fall times. A compensated (x10) oscilloscope probe will normally be required in order to minimise distortion caused by test-lead reactance. A digital storage facility can be invaluable when displaying transitory data.

Multimeters

A general-purpose multimeter can be useful when testing static line voltages, cable continuity, terminating resistances etc. A standard multi-range digital instrument will be adequate for most applications however an audible continuity testing range is useful when checking data cables.

Fault finding on RS-232 systems

Fault finding on RS-232 systems usually involves the following basic steps:

(a) ascertain which device is the DTE and which is the DCE. This can usually be accomplished by simply looking at the connectors

(DTE equipment is normally fitted with a male connector while DCE equipment is normally fitted with a female connector). Where both devices are configured as DTE (as is often the case) a patch box or null modem should be inserted for correct operation

(b) check that the correct cable has been used. Note that RS-232 cables are provided in a variety of forms; 4-way (for dumb terminals), 9-way (for normal asynchronous data communications), 15-way (for synchronous communications), and 25-way (for universal applications). If in doubt, use a full 25-way cable

(c) check that the same data word format and baud rate has been selected at each end of the serial link

(d) activate the link and investigate the logical state of the data (TXD and RXD) and handshaking (RTS, CTS etc) signal lines using a line monitor, breakout box, or interface tester. Lines may be looped back to test each end of the link

(e) if in any doubt, refer to the equipment manufacturer's data in order to ascertain whether any special connections are required and to ensure that the interfaces are truly compatible. Note that some manufacturers have implemented quasi-RS-232 interfaces which make use of TTL signals. These are *not* electrically compatible with the normal RS-232 system

(f) the communications software should be initially configured for the least complex protocol (eg, basic ASCII character transfer without handshaking). When a successful link has been established, more complex protocols may be attempted.

The program listing shows a simple GWBASIC program which can be used to test an asynchronous RS-232 link in full-duplex mode between two PCs (or PC compatibles). Similar programs can be used in other environments or between two quite different machines. The two computers should be linked using a null-modem cable (or null-modem connector) and the program should be entered, saved to disk, and then loaded and run on both computers.

The program can be easily modified to test the COM2 asynchronous port (rather than COM1) by changing the OPEN statement in line 150. This line may also be modified in order to test the link at different baud rates (other than 300 baud) and with different data formats. The OPEN command has the following syntax when used with a communications device:

OPEN "COMn: [speed],[parity],[data],[stop]" AS #filenum

where:

n	refers to the asynchronous port number (1, 2, 3, etc)
speed	is the baud rate (150, 300, 600, etc)
parity	is the parity selected (N = none, E = even, and O = odd)
data	refers to the number of data bits (5, 6, 7 or 8)
stop	refers to the number of stop bits (1, 1.5 or 2)

Readers are advised to consult the appropriate Microsoft GWBASIC or QuickBASIC manuals for further information.

```
100    REM Simple full duplex communications
105    REM test routine using PC COM1 serial port.
110    REM Data format; 300 baud, even parity,
115    REM seven data bits, one stop bit
120    KEY OFF
130    CLS
140    PRINT "GWBASIC full duplex communications"
```

```
150    OPEN "COM1:300,E,7,1" AS #1
160    K$ = INKEY$
170    IF K$ = " " THEN GOTO 210
180    IF K$ = CHR$(3) OR K$ = CHR$(27) THEN GOTO 250
190    PRINT #1,K$;
200    PRINT K$;
210    IF EOF(1) THEN GOTO 160
220    C$ = INPUT$(LOC(1),#1)
230    PRINT C$;
240    GOTO 160
250    CLOSE #1
260    CLS
270    END
```

Communication protocols

Communication protocols are the sets of rules and formats necessary for the effective exchange of information within a data communication system. The three elements of a communication protocol are *syntax* (data format, coding, and signal level definitions), *semantics* (synchronization, control, and error handling), and *timing* (sequencing of data and choice of data rate).

Communication protocols must exist on a range of levels, from the physical interconnection at one extreme to the application responsible for generating and processing the data at the other. It is useful, therefore, to think of protocols as *layered*, with each layer interacting with the layers above and below. This is an important concept and one which leads directly to the ISO seven-layered model for OSI.

ISO model for open systems interconnection

The International Standards Organisation (ISO) model for open systems interconnection (OSI) has become widely accepted as defining the seven layers of protocol which constitute a communication system.

1. Physical layer
The physical layer describes the physical circuits which provide a means of transmitting information between two users. The physical layer is concerned with such items as line voltage levels and pin connections

2. Data link layer
The data link layer defines protocols for transferring messages between the host and network and vice versa. The layer is also responsible for flow control, error detection and link management

3. Network layer
The network layer supports network connections and routing between two hosts and allows multiplexing of several channels via a common physical connection

4. Transport layer
The transport layer provides for the transparent transfer of data

between end systems which might, for example, organize data differently

5. Session layer

The session layer supports the establishment, control and termination of dialogues between application processes. The layer facilitates full duplex operation and maintains continuity of session connections. It also supports synchronization between users' equipment and generally manages the exchange of data

6. Presentation layer

The presentation layer resolves the differences in representation of information used by the application task so that each task can communicate without knowing the representation of information used by a different task (eg, different data syntax)

7. Application layer

The application layer is the ultimate source and sink for data exchange. It provides the actual user information processing function and application specific services by translating user requests into specific network functions

NB: Layers 1 to 3 of the ISO model are often referred to as *communication-oriented* layers. Layers 5 to 7, on the other hand, are referred to as *application-oriented*. In this context, the fourth layer can be thought of as a bridge between the communication and application-oriented layers of the ISO model

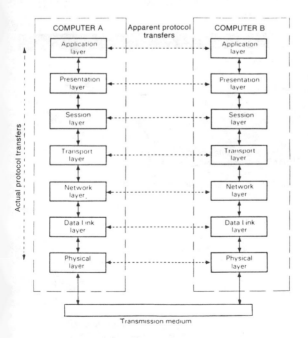

Flow control

Flow control is required in a data communications system in order to:

(a) ensure that transmission rates match the processing capabilities at each end of the link
(b) ensure that the capacity of buffer storage is not exceeded by the volume of incoming data.

Various protocols are in common use including XMODEM, YMODEM, and Kermit. Many communications software packages support several of these protocols and allow users to select that which is employed.

X-ON/X-OFF flow control

X-ON/X-OFF flow control is commonly used for serial data communications in conjunction with peripherals such as modems and serial printers. To stop a host from sending, the receiving device (peripheral) sends an X-OFF code. The host then waits until the receiving device generates an X-ON code before transmitting further serial data. X-OFF is equivalent to CTRL-S (ASCII 13 hexadecimal) whilst X-ON is equivalent to CTRL-Q (ASCII 11 hexadecimal).

XMODEM protocol

Definitions

	Meaning	Hexadecimal
SOH	start of heading	01
EOT	end of transmission	04
ACK	acknowledge	06
NAK	negative acknowledge	15
CAN	cancel	18

Transmission medium level protocol

Asynchronous data transmission with eight data bits, no parity bit, and one stop bit. The protocol imposes no restrictions on the contents of the data being transmitted. No control characters are looked for in the 128-byte data message blocks. Data may be transmitted in any form (binary, ASCII etc). The protocol may be used in a 7-bit environment for the transmission of ASCII-encoded data.

To maintain compatability with CP/M file structure and hence allow ASCII files to be transferred to and from CP/M systems, the following recommendations have been made:

(a) ASCII tab characters (09 hexadecimal) should be set every eight character positions
(b) lines should be terminated by a CR-LF combination (0D hexadecimal followed by 0A hexadecimal)
(c) end-of-file should be indicated by CTRL-Z (1A hexadecimal)
(d) variable length data is divided into 128-byte blocks for transmission purposes
(e) if the data ends on a 128-byte boundary (ie, a CR-LF combination occurs in the 127th and 128th byte positions of a block) a subsequent block containing CTRL-Z should preferably be appended in order to indicate the end-of-file (EOF)
(f) the last block transmitted is not shortened (ie, all blocks have a length of 128 bytes – there is no *short block*).

Character

File level protocol

The XMODEM file level protocol involves the following considerations:

(a) all errors are retried ten times
(b) some versions of the protocol use CAN (CTRL-X) to abort transmission. Unfortunately, such a scheme can result in premature termination of a transmission due to corruption of data bytes (which may be falsely read as CAN)
(c) the receiver will *timeout* after ten seconds and then send a NAK character. The timeout sequence should be repeated every ten seconds until the transmitter is ready to resume the transmission of data. When receiving a block, the time out is reduced to one second for each character.

The following example shows how the XMODEM protocol provides for error recovery:

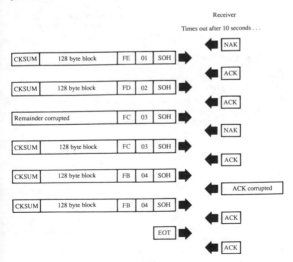

Message block level protocol

Each block transferred comprises:

SOH	blk #	255-blk #	128 data bytes	cksum

where:

SOH	is the start of heading character (01 hexadecimal)
blk #	is the block number (in pure binary) which starts at 1. The block number is incremented for each 128-byte block transmitted and wraps round from 255 to 0 (not from 255 to 1)
255-blk #	is the one's complement of the block number
cksum	is the sum of the data bytes within the 128-byte block (any carry is discarded).

Notes:

1. All single byte values are given in hexadecimal
2. SOH = 01, EOT = 04, ACK = 06, NAK = 15 (all hexadecimal).

XMODEM/CRC protocol

An improved version of XMODEM protocol exists in which the simple single byte checksum is replaced by a two-byte *cyclic redundancy check* (CRC) character. The CRC provides a more robust form of error detection

SOH	blk #	255-blk #	128 data bytes	CRC hi	CRC lo

where:

SOH	is the start of heading character (01 hexadecimal)
blk #	is the block number (in pure binary) which starts at 1. The block number is incremented for each 128-byte block transmitted and wraps round from 255 to 0 (not from 255 to 1)
255-blk #	is the one's complement of the block number
CRC hi	is the high byte of the CRC
CRC lo	is the low byte of the CRC.

The sixteen bits of the CRC are considered to be the coefficients of a polynomial. The 128-byte value of the data block is first multiplied by x^{16} and then divided by the generator polynomial $(x^{16} + x^{12} + x^5 + 1)$ using modulo-2 arithmetic ($x = 2$). The remainder of the division is the desired CRC which is then appended to the block. The CRC calculation is repeated at the receiving end, dividing the 130-byte value formed from the 128-byte data block and two-byte CRC. If anything other than a zero results as the remainder generated by this calculation, an error must have occured in which case a NAK will be generated in order to signal the need for retransmission of the block.

The file level protocol of XMODEM/CRC is similar to that used in the basic XMODEM specification with the exception that a C (43 hexadecimal) is initially transmitted by the receiver. This character is sent in place of the initial NAK. If the sender is set up to accept the modified protocol, it will respond by sending the first message block just as if a NAK had been received. If, however, it is not set up for the modified protocol, the sender will ignore the character. The receiver will then wait for 3 seconds and if no SOH character is detected, it will assume that XMODEM/CRC protocol is not available and will resume the data transfer by sending a NAK and adopting XMODEM protocol with a checksum for error detection.

The following examples shows how the XMODEM/CRC protocol provides data transfer:

(a) with a sender set up for XMODEM/CRC

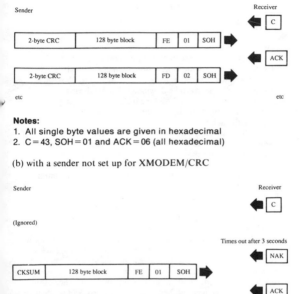

etc   etc

Notes:
1. All single byte values are given in hexadecimal
2. C = 43, SOH = 01 and ACK = 06 (all hexadecimal)

(b) with a sender not set up for XMODEM/CRC

Sender   Receiver

(Ignored)

Times out after 3 seconds

| CKSUM | 128 byte block | FE | 01 | SOH |

| CKSUM | 128 byte block | FD | 02 | SOH |

etc   etc

Notes:
1. All single byte values are given in hexadecimal
2. C = 43, SOH = 01, NAK = 15, ACK = 06 (all hexadecimal)

Kermit

Kermit is a packet-orientated file transfer protocol which was developed by Bill Catchings and Frank da Cruz at the Columbia University Centre for Computing Activities (CUCCA). The initial objective was to allow users of DEC-20 and IBM timesharing systems to archive their files on microcomputer floppy disks. The design owes much to the ANSI and ISO models and ideas were incorporated from similar projects at Stanford University and the University of Utah.

Kermit has grown to support over fifty different operating systems and is now in constant use at many sites all over the world. Kermit software is free and available to all but, to defray costs of media, printing and postage etc, a distribution fee is requested from sites that order Kermit directly from the University of Columbia. Other sites are, however, free to distribute Kermit on their own terms subject to certain stipulations.

Further details can be obtained from:

Kermit distribution,
Columbia University Centre for Computing Activities,
7th Floor Watson Laboratory,
612 West 115th Street,
New York,
NY 10025

Prospective microcomputer Kermit users should note that CUCCA can only provide 9-inch tapes (usually 1600 bit in^{-1}). Bootstrapping procedures are, however, provided to allow microcomputer versions to be downloaded from the mainframe for which the tape is produced. The tape includes all source programs and documentation. One copy of the Kermit manual is also provided with each tape.

Kermit is designed for the transfer of character-orientated sequential files over ordinary serial telecommunication lines. It is not necessarily better than many other terminal-orientated file transfer protocols but it is free, well documented, and has been implemented on a wide variety of microcomputers, minicomputers and mainframes.

Kermit transfers data by encapsulating it in packets of control information which incorporates a synchronization marker, packet number (to facilitate detection of 'lost' packets), length indicator, and a checksum to allow verification of the data. Retransmission is requested when lost or corrupt data packets are detected; duplicate packets are simply discarded. In addition, special control packets allow co-operating Kermits to connect and disconnect from each other and to exchange various kinds of information. Very few assumptions are made concerning the capabilities of either of the participating computers and hence the Kermit protocol is effective with many different types of system.

Connections between systems are established by the user. In a typical case, the user runs Kermit on a microcomputer, enters terminal emulation mode, connects to a remote host computer, logs in, runs Kermit on the remote host, and then issues commands to the remote Kermit to start a file transfer. The user then 'escapes' back to the microcomputer and issues commands to the local Kermit to commence its part of the file transfer. Files may be transferred singly or in groups.

Basic Kermit protocol provides only for transfer of sequential files, though the protocol attempts to cater for various types of sequential file. Microcomputer Kermit implementations must, of course, provide terminal emulation facilities in order to make the initial connection with the remote host.

More advanced implementations simplify the user interface by allowing the remote host's Kermit to act as a *file server* which can transfer files in either direction to, or from, the local Kermit. Servers also provide a range of additional facilities including file management, messaging etc. Other optional features include a variety of block checks, a mechanism which supports 8-bit data on a communication link set up for 7-bit operation, and methods for data compression.

Kermit protocol requires that:

(a) the host can send and receive 7- or 8-bit ASCII-encoded data over an RS-232 physical connection (either hard-wired or dialup)
(b) printable ASCII characters are not transformed in any way
(c) a single ASCII control character passes from one system to the other without transformation. This character is used for packet synchronization and is normally SOH (ie, CTRL-A). The character may, however, be redefined if required
(d) the host line terminator must be a single ASCII control character (such as CR or LF) distinct from the packet synchronization character
(e) the Kermit program must be allowed to set up a job's controlling terminal for raw binary data (ie, there must be no insertion of CR-LF characters nor formatting of incoming or outgoing characters,
(f) the host's terminal input processor must be capable of handling Kermit packets which comprise bursts of typically between 40 and 100 characters at normal transmission speeds.

Kermit does not require that:

(a) a particular transmission speed or baud rate is available
(b) X-ON/X-OFF or any other kind of flow control is available
(c) full-duplex operation is supported. Any mixture of half or full-duplex operation is supported
(d) a system supports full 8-bit byte operation. Kermit will take full advantage of an 8-bit system to transmit binary files encoded as 8-bit bytes but, when a system does not allow this mode of operation, an optional encoding prefix is used.

Kermit transactions

The Kermit file transfer protocol involves a *transaction* in which an exchange of packets begins with a *send-init* (S) packet and ends with a *break transmission* (B) or *error* (E) packet. The transaction may include the transfer of one or more files, all in the same direction. The following diagram illustrates a Kermit transaction:

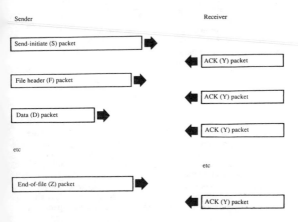

The send-initiate packet and its corresponding ACK (Y) response are responsible for setting the parameter used in the ensuing exchange. Each packet has a sequence number (starting with 0 for the initial send-initiate packet). The acknowledgment (ACK or NAK) for the packet has the same packet number as the packet being acknowledged. When a successful acknowledgement (ACK) is received, the modulo-64 packet number is incremented.

If a fatal error is detected, an error (E) packet is generated which contains a brief text message in the data field. This message is printed on the console before the system reverts to command mode.

Kermit packet format
Note that all fields consist of ASCII characters

MARK	char(LEN)	char(SEQ)	TYPE	DATA	CHECK

where:

MARK is the synchronization character (normally SOH or CTRL-A)

char(LEN) is a single character which represents the number of characters which follow (ie, the packet length minus 2). The length does not include end-of-line or padding characters but it does include the block check characters. The char() function transforms an integer which is assumed to lie in the range 0 to 94 into a printable ASCII character. The conversion function is: char(x) = x + 32

char(SEQ) is a single character which represents the modulo-64 packet sequence number. Sequence numbers wrap around to 0 when the count advances beyond 63. The char() function is again used to transform the number so that it appears as a printable ASCII character

TYPE is the packet type indicated by a single ASCII character

Packet type	Character
Data	D
Error	E
Acknowledge	Y(ACK)
Negative acknowledge	N(NAK)
Send-initiate	S
Break transmission	B(EOT)
File header	F
End-of-file	Z(EOF)
Reserved (eg, for timeout)	T

DATA is the data to be transmitted (where applicable). ASCII control characters (ie, those in the range 0 to 31) are preceded by a special character (normally #) and modified so that they become printable ASCII characters using the ctl() function
ctl(x) = x XOR 64

CHECK is a block check character on the characters in the packet (but not including the MARK and CHECK characters themselves). The check for each packet is computed at both ends and must agree if the packet is to be accepted. A single character arithmetic checksum is used of which only six bits of the arithmetic sum are used. In order that all of the bits of each data character contribute to this quantity, bits 6 and 7 of the final value are added to the quantity formed by bits 0 to 5. Kermit's default block check is formed according to the rule

CHECK = char((s + ((s AND 192)/64)) AND 63)

where s is the arithmetic sum of the ASCII characters within the packet.

Kermit commands

(a) Basic commands

Command	Function
SEND	tells Kermit to send one or more files
RECEIVE	tells Kermit to expect one or more files to arrive
GET	tells a user Kermit to send one or more files. (NB some Kermits use the RECEIVE command for both RECEIVE and GET functions and this often causes some confusion)

The above commands take operands which are file specifications. If desired, different file specifications can be used for the local and remote files and optional operands have been shown in brackets in the example here

SEND local-source-filespec [remote-destination-filespec]
RECEIVE [local-destination-filespec]
GET remote-source-filespec [local-destination-filespec]

(b) Program management commands

Command	Function
EXIT	exits the Kermit program with 'clean-up'
LOG	specifies a log for file transactions or for terminal session log in
PUSH	preserves the current Kermit environment and enters the system command processor
QUIT	exits the Kermit program without 'clean-up'
TAKE	reads and executes Kermit program commands taken from a local file

(c) Terminal emulation commands

Command	Function
COMMAND	instructs the local Kermit to enter terminal emulation mode. The local system will then appear as a terminal connected to the remote system. An escape character is provided so that the user can get back to the local system. The escape character takes a single character argument

Argument	Function
0	transmit a NUL
B	transmit a BREAK
C	close the connection and return to Kermit command level
P	push to system command processor
Q	quit logging (if applicable)
R	resume logging
S	show status of a connection
?	show the available command (Note that the escape character may be followed by a second escape character when it is necessary to transmit the escape character itself)

(d) Special user-mode commands

Command	Function
BYE	instructs a remote server to log itself out and, upon successful completion, terminate the local Kermit program
FINISH	instructs a remote server to shut itself down without logging out. The local Kermit is left at command level so that the user can later re-CONNECT to the remote job

(e) File management commands

The commands are a selection of those which are provided in Kermit implementations which support file management

Command	Function
COPY	make a copy of the specified file using the specified new name
DELETE	delete the specified file
DIRECTORY	list the names and attributes of the files within the current working directory
PRINT	dump the specified file to the line printer
RENAME	rename the specified file using the specified new name
SHOW	display current configuration (ie, settings of parameters)
SUBMIT	submit the specified line for background processing
TYPE	display the contents of the specified file at the terminal

(f) Configuration commands

Command	Function
SET	configure the system for a particular set of parameters. Allowable parameters will vary with a particular implementation but should normally include block checking, duplex mode, flow control, maximum packet length, parity, timeout period etc

A macro facility is highly desirable in order to simplify use of the SET command. The following is a typical macro definition for use in conjunction with SET

**DEFINE IBM = PARITY ODD, DUPLEX HALF,
HANDSHAKE XON**

Thereafter, a command of the form

SET IBM

could be used to select odd parity, half-duplex operation, and enable X-ON/X-OFF handshaking.

CCITT X.25

CCITT X.25 is a major protocol standard which has gained much support amongst computer and networks vendors alike. X.25 originated in 1976 (before the emergence of the ISO model for OSI) and thus it is perhaps not surprising that it does not conform exactly to this widely accepted model. In 1983, the US Government adopted a subset of X.25 for use by federal departments and agencies. This joint standard appears in Federal Information Processing Standard (FIPS) 100/Federal Standard (FED-STD) 1041

X.25 corresponds to the lower layers of the ISO model (with some overlap) as shown below:

ISO layer

X.25

7	Application
6	Presentation
5	Session
4	Transport
3	Network
2	Data link
1	Physical

3	Packet level
2	Link level
1	Physical level

X.25 is best described as a *packet mode interface protocol* which also offers some end-to-end properties. X.25 has the following major characteristics:

Physical level

Transmission rates:	2.4 K, 4.8 K and 9.6 K bps
Interface requirements:	RS-232, X21, RS-449

Link level

Procedure:	linked access protocol (LAP) and link access protocol balanced (LAPB)
Maximum outstanding data frames:	7
Maximum number of bits per information frame:	164 octets

Packet level

Services:	virtual call and permanent virtual circuit
Packet types:	all basic types plus diagnostic packets
User data-field length:	integral number of octets
Packet sequence numbering:	modulo-8
Delivery confirmation:	supported by all DCE (DTE need not employ the delivery confirmation bit when sending to the DCE)
Fast select:	a DCE should implement fast select (a DTE need not employ fast select when sending to a DCE).

X.25 packet format

The general format of an X.25 packet is shown below:

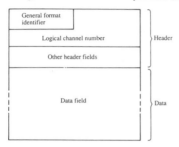

The general format identifier occupies the four most significant bits of the first octet and the logical channel number comprises group and channel numbers in the four least significant bits of the first octet and eight bits of the second octet respectively. The remainder of the header contains various items of information depending upon the type of packet.

X.25 control packet format

0 0 0 1	Group number	
Channel number		
Command type		1
Calling DTE address length	Called DTE address length	
DTE address		
	0 0 0 0	
0 0	Facility length	
Facilities		
User data		

X.25 data packet format

Q	D	01	Group number

Channel number

Ack. number	M	Sequence number	O

User data

Notes:

1. The Q bit (MSB of first octet) provides a mechanism by which the user may operate two streams of data across a single virtual circuit. If this facility is not used, the Q bit defaults to 0. The Q bit is set to 1 when messages are sent to the packet assembly/disassembly (PAD) device. Packets destined for a terminal (or assembled by a PAD from a terminal) have the Q bit reset (ie, 0).

2. The D bit is set to logic 1 in order to indicate that immediate confirmation of packet receipt is required (rather than waiting until a window is full). In the call set-up routine, the D bit may be set by the sender to ascertain whether the receiver can support this feature. The response is indicated by the state of the D bit within the call accept packet.

High-level data link control

High-level data link control (HDLC) is a synchronous communication protocol on which many of today's LAN protocols are based. HDLC is a *bit-oriented protocol*; the bit representation of the data in the form of characters, binary numbers, or decimal numbers, is contained wholly within the data field of a single frame.

HDLC provides three classes of procedure for network connection between adjacent nodes in a point-to-point communication system .

Asynchronous balanced mode

Asynchronous balanced mode (ABM) relates to full duplex communication between two nodes who are considered to be 'equal partners' in the data exchange. Both can initiate and terminate a connection and both can send data (without prior interrogation) on an established connection.

Normal response mode

Normal response mode (NRM) relates to communication between a control device (eg, a computer) and a number of secondary stations.

Asynchronous response mode

Asynchronous response mode (ARM) relates to communication in half-duplex mode between a primary station which sends out commands and data and a secondary station which returns responses.

HDLC frame structure

A number of fields are employed within an HDLC frame, including:

Flag

The flag is used for synchronization and also indicates the start (*preamble*) and end (*postamble*) of the frame. The flag takes the form: 01111110, and this pattern is avoided in the data field by a technique known as *bit stuffing*.

Bit stuffing is the name given to a process in which the transmitter automatically inserts an extra 0 bit after each occurrence of five 1 bits in the data being transmitted. When the receiver detects a sequence of five 1 bits, it examines the next bit. If this bit is a 0, the receiver deletes it. However, if this bit is a 1, it indicates that the bit pattern must form part of preamble or postamble code.

Address

Identifies the sending or receiving station.

Control

The control frame is used to identify one of three different types of frame:
(a) information frame (the frame contains data)
(b) supervisory frame (the frame provides basic link control functions)
(c) un-numbered frame (the frame provides supplementary link control functions)

Data

The data frame contains the data to be transmitted.

Frame check sequence

The frame check sequence (FCS) comprises a 16-bit *cyclic redundancy check* (CRC) which is calculated from the contents of the address, control, and data fields.

HDLC frame structure

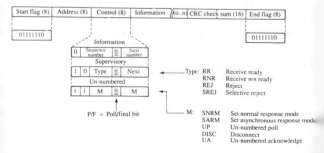

Local area networks

A local area network (LAN) is a network which covers a limited area and which generally provides a high data rate capability. A LAN is invariably confined to a single site (ie, a building or group of buildings) and provides for the exchange of information and efficient use of shared resources within the site.

In general a LAN should:

- conform to a well defined international standard supported by a number of manufacturers and vendors
- support a high data rate (typically 1 to 10 Mbps)
- have a maximum range of typically at least 500 metres and, in some cases, as much as 10 km
- be capable of supporting a variety of hardware independent devices (connected as *nodes*)
- provide high standards of reliability and data integrity
- exhibit minimal reliance on centralised components and controlling elements
- maintain performance under conditions of high loading
- allow easy installation and expansion
- readily permit maintenance, reconfiguration, and expansion.

LAN topology

Local area networks are often categorised in terms of the topology which they employ. The following topologies are commonly encountered; *star, ring, tree,* and *bus* (the latter is a tree which has only one *trunk* and no *branches*).

In star topology, a central switching element is used to connect all of the nodes within the network. A node wishing to transmit data to another node must initiate a request to the central switching element which will then provide a dedicated path between them, once the circuit has been established, the two nodes may communicate as if they were connected by a dedicated point-to-point path.

Ring topology is characterised by a closed loop to which each node is attached by means of a repeating element. Data circulates around the ring on a series of point-to-point links which exist between the repeaters. A node wishing to transmit must wait for its turn and then send data onto the ring in the form of a *packet* which must contain both the source and destination addresses as well as the data itself. Upon arrival at the destination node, the data is copied into a local buffer. The packet continues to circulate until it returns to the source node, hence providing a form of acknowledgement.

Bus and tree topologies both employ a multiple-access broadcast medium and hence only one device can transmit at any time. As with ring topology, transmission involves the generation of a packet containing source and destination address field together with data.

Star LAN topology

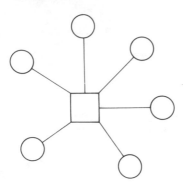

Ring LAN topology

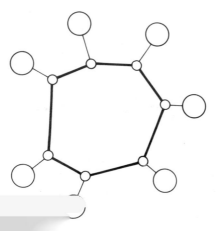

ogy

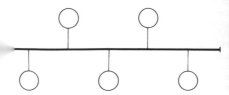

~ee LAN topology

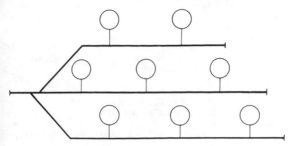

Key

Controlling/switching element

Node (eg computer)

Medium access unit, transceiver etc

Node access cable, transceiver drop etc

Transmission medium (shared)

Transmission medium with termination

Broadband and baseband transmission

Local area networks are available which support either *broadband* or *baseband* transmission. In the former case, information is modulated onto a radio frequency carrier which is passed through the transmission medium (eg, coaxial cable). In the latter case, digital information is passed directly through the transmission medium. It is important to note that broadband LANs can exploit frequency division multiplexing which allows a number of modulated radio frequency carriers (each with its own digital signal) to be simultaneously present within the transmission medium. Baseband LANs can only support one information signa at a time within the transmission medium.

IEEE 802 standards

The IEEE Local Network Standards Committee has developed a series of standards for local area networks. These standards have been produced with reference to the ISO model for OSI and they are summarised here:

General management, addressing and internetworking

IEEE 802.1 (Part A) Overview and architecture.

IEEE 802.1 (Part B) Addressing, internetworking, and network management.

Logical link control

IEEE 802.2 Logical link control (LLC) employed in conjunction with the four media access standards defined under IEEE 802.3, 802.4, 802.5, and 802.6.

Media access control

IEEE 802.3 Carrier sense multiple access and collision detection (CSMA/CD) access method and physical layer specifications.

Note: The European Computer Manufacturers' Association (ECMA) has produced a set of standards which bears a close relationship to that of IEEE 802.3. ECMA standards 80, 81, and 82 relate to CSMA/CD baseband LAN coaxial cables, physical layer, and link layer respectively

IEEE 802.4 Token-passing bus access method and physical layer specifications.

IEEE 802.5 Token-passing ring access method and physical layer specifications.

IEEE 802.6 Metropolitan network access method and physical layer specifications.

Relationship between IEEE 802 standards and the ISO model

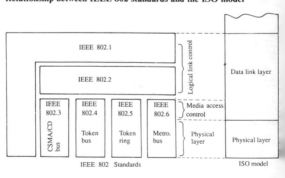

IEEE 802 Standards   ISO model

Typical LAN selection flowchart

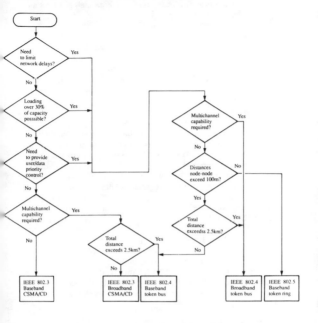

Popular network standards

Ethernet

The Ethernet standard follows IEEE 802.3 and has been widely
accepted by a number of independent systems suppliers and is
supported by Digital Equipment Corporation (DEC), Intel, and
Xerox. Ethernet's popularity stems from a number of factors
including the availability of VLSI controllers which permit cost-
effective implementation of a network and the high data rate of 10
Mbps.

The Ethernet link control layer employs carrier sense multiple
access with collision detection (CSMA/CD) and an HDLC-type
frame structure is employed. Basic network physical layer
components comprise coaxial cables for transmission media
(maximum segment length 500 metres), transceivers with collision
detection circuitry, a transceiver drop cable (maximum length 50
metres) which connects data terminal equipment to a nearby
transceiver unit, and a controller board. This latter device is
responsible for frame assembly/disassembly, handling source and
destination addressing, detection of physical transmission errors,
collision detection and retransmission.

Where network distances are to exceed 500 metres, multiple segments are employed and these are linked by means of repeaters. Point-to-point links are used to link together segments which are separated by physical distances of up to 1 km. Such links act as a repeater divided into two sections.

Cheapernet

Cheapernet also follows IEEE 802.3 but provides a low-cost alternative to Ethernet in which the transceiver function is incorporated within the terminal equipment (the cable tap box and transceiver cable are thus no longer required). Savings in cost are also made by using lower grade coaxial cable throughout the network and terminal equipment is simply attached using T-connectors at strategic points. Cheapernet is thus very much simpler to install than its more expensive counterpart.

The limitations of Cheapernet are that its segment length is restricted to 185 metres (making repeaters essential for larger networks) and that the IEEE 802.3 cable/terminal ground isolation scheme (which requires d.c. isolation between transceiver and terminal) is not so easy to implement using VLSI devices when the transceiver function is to be integrated within the controller. These two drawbacks can seriously limit the cost-effectiveness of the system when compared with a full Ethernet implementation of IEEE 802.3.

Baseband IBM PC LAN

The baseband IBM PC LAN allows a mixture of PCs and PS/2 machines to communicate with one another at relatively low-cost. A PC network adapter/A, network support program, and PC LAN program is required at each node. CSMA/CD protocol is used and the network employs a twisted pair cable in which the data rate is 2 Mbps.

Broadband IBM PC LAN

The broadband IBM PC LAN also allows a mixture of PCs and PS/2 machines to communicate with one another with the aid of a PC network adapter II/A, network support program and PC LAN program at each node. In addition, one or more PC network translator units are required. Each translator unit can handle up to eight nodes at distances not exceeding 200 feet. Larger networks can be realised using further translators and standard IBM Cable System components. The broadband PC LAN operates at a data rate of 2 Mbps with CSMA/CD protocol and coaxial cable.

IBM Token Ring LAN

The IBM Token Ring LAN can be used to implement a larger network in which computer systems (eg, System/370) can communicate with a variety of PC and PS/2 machines. Token ring network adapters are required at each PC or PS/2 node together with one or more multi-station access units. The data transfer rate for the network is 4 Mbps.

ICL Macrolan

ICL Macrolan employs a modified form of token-passing ring which incorporates features designed to improve the efficiency and fault tolerance of the system. The system uses optical fibres as the physical medium with multi-port ring switches which permit disconnection of inactive nodes. Two optical cables are required for each node in order to permit full duplex operation.

Manufacturing Automation Protocol (MAP)
Manufacturing Automation Protocol (MAP) is a broadband token bus system which uses community television (CATV) coaxial cable as its physical medium. The standard was developed by General Motors but has become widely accepted by a number of major manufacturing and production engineering concerns as a robust and versatile factory networking standard.

The layers within MAP closely follow the ISO model for OSI (there is direct correspondence at the application, session, transport, network, data link and physical levels). The data link layer follows IEEE 802.2 while the physical layer corresponds to the IEEE 802.4 (token bus) standard. The system employs quadrature amplitude modulation (QAM) at a data rate of 10 Mbps.

Technical and Office Protocol (TOP)
Technical and Office Protocol (TOP) was developed by Boeing Computer Services and has much in common with MAP. TOP can, however, be implemented at lower cost using the CSMA/CD protocol defined under IEEE 802.3. The upper layers of TOP correspond closely to those within MAP and thus it is possible to interwork the two systems. TOP version 1.1 employs standard Ethernet trunk coaxial cable with a maximum segment length of 500 metres (adequate for most office and commercial environments). A routing device (or *router*) permits interconnection of MAP and TOP networks. The routing device essentially provides a bridge above layer of the ISO model and resolves any differences between address domains, frame sizes etc.

Summary of popular LAN specifications

Name	Supplier	LAN type	Topology	Transmission medium	Protocol	Maximum cable length	Maximum nodes	Data rate (bps)
Apple Talk	Apple Computer	Ba	Bus	T/pair	CSMA/CD	300 m	32	230
Cambridge	Camtec	Ba	Bus	T/pair F/opt	Cambridge Ring			10 M
Ethernet	various	Ba	Bus	Coax	CSMA/CD	500 m	100	10 M
FastLAN	Wang	Br	Bus	Coax	CSMA/CD	186 m		10 M
IBM PC Network	IBM	Br	Bus	Coax	CSMA/CD	300 m		2 M
Isolan	BICC	Ba	Bus	Coax	CSMA/CD	4 km		10 M
Netware	Novell	Ba	Bus/star	Coax	CSMA/CD		1024	10 M
NIM1000	Olivetti	Ba	Bus	Coax	CSMA/CD	2.5 km	100	10 M
Nimbus Network	Research Machines	Ba	Bus	Coax	CSMA/CD	1.2 km	1024	10 M
OSLAN	ICL	Ba	Bus	Coax	CSMA/CD		32 +	800
Planet	Racal-Milgo	Ba	Ring	Coax	Token	300 m	500	10 M
Primenet	Prime Computer	Ba	Ring	Coax	Cambridge Ring	2.25 km	63	10 M
WangNet	Wang	Br	Bus	Coax	CSMA/CD	13 km		10 M
X.25-based	various	Ba	Star	T/pair F/opt	X.25			64 K

Notes:
Ba = baseband   T/pair = twisted pair
Br = broadband   F/opt = fibre optic

Ethernet

Basic Ethernet connecting arrangement

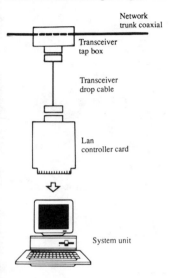

Ethernet transceiver cable pin connections

Pin number / Assignment

1 shield (also connected to connector shell)
2 collision +
3 transmit +
4 reserved
5 receive +
6 power
7 reserved
8 reserved
9 collision
10 transmit
11 reserved
12 receive
13 power +
14 reserved
15 reserved

Ethernet transceiver cable specifications

Construction:	four-pair 78 ohm differential impedance plus overall shield (eg, BICC H9600)
Loop resistance:	less than 4 ohm for power pair
Signal loss:	less than 3 dB at 10 MHz (typical maximum length equivalent 40 metres)
Connectors:	1 × female and 1 × male 15-pin D-connector.

Typical Ethernet interface configuration

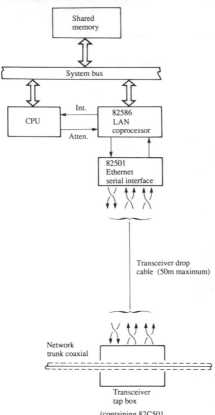

Typical Cheapernet interface configuration

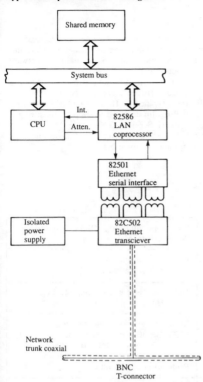

Internal architecture of the 82C502 Ethernet transceiver

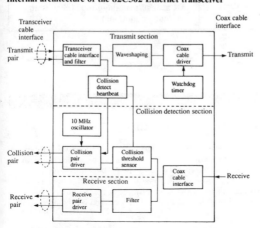

LAN software

The software required to operate a local area network successfully bridges the gaps between the session layer, presentation layer, and applications layer of the ISO model for OSI. In addition, software defined for use in conjunction with the lower layers of the model is concerned with the efficient transport of data within the LAN and for establishing the dialogue between users, servers, and other resources. Such software is typified by IBM's NETBIOS and the IBM PC LAN Support Program designed to support token ring networks and Xerox Network Services (XNS).

The relationship between the seven-layered ISO model and the categories of software present is shown below:

ISO layer	Software
7 Application	User application (eg, dBase IV, Word, WordPerfect, etc)
6 Presentation	Network operating system and LAN utilities (eg, NetWare, etc)
5 Session	Host operating system (eg, MS-DOS, OS/2, Unix, Xenix, etc)
4 Transport	Network transport systems, (eg, IBM NETBIOS, IBM PC LAN Support Program, Novell IPX, Xerox Network Service (XNS),
3 Network	Transport Control Protocol/Internet Protocol (TCP/IP), etc)
2 Data link	Link control/media access
1 Physical	LAN access/signalling (eg, Token Ring, Ethernet, Arcnet, etc)

Network operating systems

A network operating system (NOS) provides added value to an individual PC or work station by facilitating resource sharing and information transfer via the LAN. The NOS is thus crucial in determining the overall effectiveness of the system as well as the transparency of the network in terms of access to the communications, file, and print services offered by the network server.

Software architecture of a typical network work station (PC)

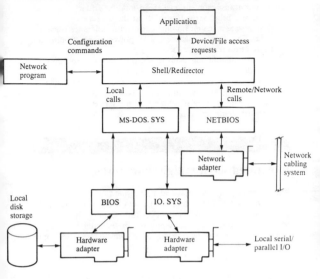

Software architecture of a typical file server

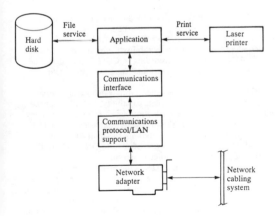

NOS facilities

In general, a network operating system should:

(a) provide access to files via the file server on a multi-tasking basis

(b) provide a user shell which, in conjunction with the host operating system (eg, MS-DOS), will redirect network file requests

(c) provide file and record locking
(d) include transaction support (read/modify/write)
(e) manage a print queue (normally at the file server)
(f) incorporate a significant element of fault tolerance (including redundant directory management, power supply monitoring, transaction tracking, etc)
(g) incorporate differing levels of security and/or access control
(h) provide network accounting facilities
(i) permit inter-networking via internal and/or external bridges (and asynchronous communications, where appropriate)
(j) incorporate message handling facilities for 'store and forward' communications.

Integrated services digital networks

The International Telegraph and Telephone Consultative Committee (CCITT) has developed a set of recommendations coordinated by its Digital Networks Study Group. The recommendations, individually prefixed by the letter *I* and collectively known as the *I series*, cover such ISDN related topics as the ISDN concept and associated principles, overall network aspects and functions, user-network interfaces and inter-network interfaces.

The 1200 and 1300 series of CCITT recommendations respectively describe the services and network capabilities provided by an ISDN while the 1100 series provide general recommendations for ISDN (including fundamental descriptions and definitions of terms).

The CCITT recommendations provide some firm definitions of static and dynamic networks as well as the ISDN itself. Furthermore, an ISDN *bearer service* is defined as a service to the customer which allows him the capability for information transfer between ISDN access points according to CCITT standards. The higher layer (ie, above layer 3) terminal functions being defined by the customer.

An ISDN *teleservice*, on the other hand, is defined as a service which allows the customer complete capability, including defined terminal equipment functions, for communications with another user of the service, according to protocols established by CCITT.

The intention of the CCITT in making this distinction between bearer and teleservices is clearly one of ensuring that technical standards are safeguarded in order to permit international interconnection; access to the ISDN being made available at different points depending upon the category of service.

When planning the ISDN it is essential to ensure that any scheme adopted offers an optimal solution in terms of future expansion and, most important of all, any decisions taken must not constrain future actions.

Any plan should bear in mind the following important considerations:

1. the system should be suitable for local, toll, and rural applications without further modification
2. the system should be modular in order to permit the addition/replacement/upgrading of capital plant and equipment as, and when, needs arise

3. system architecture should, as far as possible, be compatible with any existing network environment.

Existing networks have evolved largely through analogue technology. However, there is a pressing need for both technologies to co-exist in any future mixed analog/digital network. Unfortunately, the performance and cost parameters of purely digital networks are quite different from those of their purely analog counterparts. This, in turn, accounts for the major differences in optimal network architecture of the two types of system. Furthermore, the transition from an existing analog telephone network to a full ISDN will clearly differ from one country to another. Indeed, the type of network and rate of introduction, will depend on a number of factors paramount among which is the nature and degree of penetration of any existing digital networks.

Finally, an important, and somewhat sobering, fact of life for network planners is that equipment and line plant installed today will, during the next decade or so, be expected to handle an increasing proportion of non-voice services during its lifetime. These non-voice services can be expected to rise from around 8% of subscribers by 1990, 20% by 1995, and as much as 50% by the year 2000.

ISDN in the UK

In the UK, British Telecom's ISDN-2 provides two B channels each operating at 64 Kbps and one D channel at 16 Kbps. The B channels cater for voice and data but may be parallel configured with the use of appropriate terminal equipment to provide a single 128 Kbps channel. The D channel is primarily used for signalling between the terminal and the network but in some applications can also be used to carry packed switched data.

The BT basic rate access (BRA) service was formally launched in February 1991 and is available from most System X local exchanges. From 1992, all business users who request an additional business line (or who ask for two new business lines) from BT will have access to ISDN-2 via a network termination (NT) adapter.

Several manufacturers (including IBM and ICL) can supply ISDN PC adapter cards which have been approved specifically for the UK. BT can provide further information concerning its ISDN services by means of a freephone 'hotline' which is available on 0800-181514.

ITT System 12

System 12, the largest project ever undertaken by ITT, was initially aimed at local, toll, rural, combined local/toll, and local/tandem applications but evolution to a full ISDN was a feature of the overall design concept. Furthermore, rather than opting for a simple, yet relatively shortlived, solution based on conventional centralised stored program control of the type prevalent in existing analogue exchanges, ITT boldly opted for a system of distributed control, using modular hardware based on a specially developed range of custom VLSI devices.

Coordination of the System 12 project is vested in the International Telecommunication Centre (ITC) at Brussels but major contributions have been made by the six principal ITT design houses located in Antwerp, Harlow, Madrid, Milan, Shelton, and Stuttgart.

System 12 claims to be a 'future safe' design; accommodating change on an incremental basis as and when required. The first System 12 exchanges have now been in operation for nearly five years and, during that time, have shown some exceptionally high availabilities (more than 0.9999 in the Deutsche Bundespost exchanges).

The key to System 12's huge success is the versatility of the system inherent in the use of distributed control architecture. The system consists of a common centralised digital switching network; connected, by means of a standard interface, to a series of other modules. The digital switching network comprises a group switch (organised as a number of switching planes) together with a number of access switches. The individual service modules comprise appropriate terminal hardware together with related *terminal control elements* (TCE).

In order to provide interconnection of the terminal modules, the terminal control elements establish digital paths throughout the switching network. A digital path consists of a 16-bit timeslot with an 8 kHz repetition rate. One byte (eight bits) is available in each timeslot for external users and this results in a 64 Kbps digital path for user traffic. This, however, can be increased to $n \times 64$ Kbps, by using n multiple paths. The Deutsche Bundespost system, for example, employs values for n of 2, 4, 8, 12, 24, and 30.

The digital switching network is *end-controlled* and commands contained within the timeslot allow paths to be established between terminal modules without a central network map and path search mechanism. This concept provides virtually limitless expansion of the system in terms of the number of terminals and TCE which can be provided.

The dimensions of the group switch are determined by the overall size of the system and the volume of switched traffic. System size is primarily determined by the number of digital network access switches. In turn, this determines whether one, two, or three group switching stages are required. The volume of switched traffic, on the other hand, determines the number of planes (two, three, or four) required within the group switch.

The terminal control element comprises three hardware blocks (terminal interface, microprocessor, and memory) linked together by means of a high speed bus. The TCE is connected to both the terminal circuits and the digital switching network via two bi-directional 32-channel PCM links. Since each timeslot contains 16 bits and the repetition rate for a frame comprising 32 individual timeslots is 8 kHz, the PCM links run at $(16 \times 32 \times 8)$ Kbps or 4.096 Mbps. Thirty of the 32 channels are available for user traffic (PCM voice or data) with the remaining two channels employed, as usual, for PCM synchronisation control. An input is also provided to the TCE for up to 32 PCM encoded tone or voice announcement sources which are located in a dedicated clock and tone module.

The TCE microprocessor can establish a unidirectional digital path from the terminal interface through the digital switching network to a second terminal interface and microprocessor which can, in turn, establish a return path back to the first microprocessor. These two paths can be used for the exchange of messages between participating TCE. The TCE microprocessor can also establish digital paths between any channels of the incoming and outgoing PCM links connected to the terminal interface. This permits switching user traffic to or from the digital switching network. Bidirectional traffic between two subscribers requires two unidirectional paths to be established through the digital switching network.

Depending upon the type of service provided, individual modules will, of course, have different terminal hardware and TCE software. The TCE software usually comprises the operating system, call handling, telephonic support, and maintenance and control programs. Each TCE also contains appropriate applications programs specific to the particular module.

System 12 uses five call processing functions dealing with signal processing (F1), call control (F2), resource management (F3), translations (F4) and switching network control (F5). It is important to note that, within the distributed control structure, none of these functions is entrusted to a single microcomputing element!

Crucial to the evolution of System 12 to a full ISDN is the fact that all System 12 modules contain their own control elements and, furthermore, the handling of calls originating from a particular module involves only a few other control elements. This makes it feasible to have different module and control element types, containing software appropriate to particular types of user. Hence, within the same exchange, conventional telephony subscriber modules can coexist with ISDN subscriber modules. Little interaction is required between these two quite different types of module apart from the obvious requirement to establish voice calls between the two.

Future developments in ISDN

The obvious next stage of development in the evolution of the ISDN is the provision of services such as high speed data transmission and high resolution television. Unfortunately, such services require very high bit rates and consequently demand excessive bandwidths within the transmission medium.

To illustrate this point, a minimum bit rate of approximately 2 Mbps is considered appropriate for high speed data and document transmission whereas, for high definition TV a minimum bit rate of 140 Mbps is considered necessary. To accommodate these new services, subscribers' access lines will require comparably wide bandwidths.

Within the transit network, however, special coding techniques can be employed in order to reduce the cost overhead associated with wideband long distance transmission. For video telephony and video conferencing, it would then be possible to reduce the transit network bit rate to around one third of that present within the subscribers' access lines.

The Deustche Bundespost is currently planning a nationwide wideband satellite system based on ITT System 12 exchanges which will switch data at a rate of 1.920 Mbps. Other data services operating at this rate will undoubtedly become operational within the next year, or so, in several European countries.

ISDN can also be expected to have a major effect on the introduction of wide area networks (WAN) which are currently used primarily as a means of interconnecting remotely sited local area networks (LAN). The ISDN is eminently suited to this same task but offers improved reliability together with reduced capital costs and overheads. Hence, provided that an ISDN is in existence at each site, the need for a WAN can be eliminated.

Data cable types

Many different types of cable are employed in data communications ranging from simple twisted-pair to multi-core coaxial. For uncritical applications where speed and distance are both limited, twisted-pair cables are perfectly adequate. However, for more critical applications which involve high data rates and longer distances, high quality low-loss coaxial cables are essential. Furthermore, to minimise the effects of crosstalk, induced noise and radiation, individual and overall braided or foil screens may be required. The following diagrams (courtesy of BICC) are provided in order to assist readers in identifying the major types of cable which are in current use.

Multi-core (unscreened)

Multi-core with overall braid screen

Multi-core with individually screened conductors

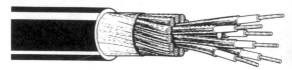

Two-pair cable with overall braid screen

Single-pair cable with foil screen

Two-pair cable with overall braid and foil screens (stranded signal conductors)

Two-pair cable with overall braid and foil screens (solid signal conductors)

Multi-pair cable with overall foil screen

Multi-pair cable with individual foil screens

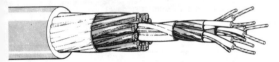

Multi-pair cable with overall braid and foil screens

Coaxial cable with foil and braid screens

Coaxial cable with double braid screen and foil (Ethernet trunk)

Multi-pair with individual foil and overall braid screens (Ethernet transceiver drop)

Two-pair with individual foil and overall braid screens (IBM indoor data cable)

Four-pair with individual foil and overall foil and braid screens (DECconnect transceiver cable)

Four-pair unscreened (DECconnect four-pair cable)

Flat six-way unscreen (DECconnect cordage)

Coaxial cable with braid screen and solid centre conductor

Dual coaxial cable with individual braid screens and solid centre conductors

Coaxial cable with double braid screens

Simplex optical cable

Duplex optical cable

Coaxial cable data

Type	Centre conductor	Diameter (mm)	Impedance (ohm)	Capacitance (pF m^{-1})	Attenuation (dB m^{-1})
RG6/U	1/1.02 mm	6.86	75	56.8	0.069 at 100 MHz
RG11A/U	7/0.41 mm	10.3	75	67	
RG58C/U	19/0.18 mm	4.95	50	100	0.2 at 10 MHz
					0.31 at 200 MHz
					0.76 at 1 GHz
RG59B/U	1/0.58 mm	6.15	75	60.6	0.12 at 100 MHz
					0.19 at 200 MHz
					0.3 at 400 MHz
					0.46 at 1 GHz
RG59/U	1/0.64 mm	6.15	75	56.8	0.098 at 100 MHz
RG62A/U	1/0.64 mm	6.15	93	36	0.26 at 400 MHz
RG174/U	1/0.4 mm	2.56	60	101	0.292 at 100 MHz
RG174A/U	7/0.16 mm	2.54	50	100	0.11 at 10 MHz
					0.42 at 200 MHz
					0.67 at 400 MHz
RG178B/U	7/0.1 mm	1.91	50	106	0.18 at 10 MHz
					0.44 at 100 MHz
					0.95 at 400 MHz
					1.4 at 1 GHz
RG179B/U	7/0.1 mm	2.54	75	66	0.19 at 10 MHz
					0.32 at 100 MHz
					0.69 at 400 MHz
					0.82 at 1 GHz
RG188A/U	7/0.17 mm	2.6	50	93	
RG213/U	7/0.029 mm	10.29	50	98	0.18 at 400 MHz
RG214/U	7/0.029 mm	10.79	50	98	0.18 at 400 MHz
RG223/U	1/0.9 mm	5.5	50	96	
RG316/U	7/0.17 mm	2.6	50	102	
URM43	1/0.9 mm	5	50	100	0.13 at 100 MHz
					0.187 at 200 MHz
					0.232 at 300 MHz
					0.338 at 600 MHz
					0.446 at 1 GHz
URM57	1/1.15 mm	10.3	75	67	0.061 at 100 MHz
					0.09 at 200 MHz
					0.113 at 300 MHz
					0.17 at 600 MHz
					0.231 at 1 GHz
URM67	7/0.77 mm	10.3	50	100	0.068 at 100 MHz
					0.099 at 200 MHz
					0.125 at 300 MHz
					0.186 at 500 MHz
					0.252 at 1 GHz
URM70	7/0.19 mm	5.8	75	67	0.152 at 100 MHz
					0.218 at 200 MHz
					0.27 at 300 MHz
					0.391 at 600 MHz
					0.517 at 1 GHz

Type	Centre conductor	Diameter (mm)	Impedance (ohm)	Capacitance (pF m⁻¹)	Attenuation (dB m⁻¹)
URM76	7/0.32 mm	5	50	100	0.155 at 100 MHz
					0.222 at 200 MHz
					0.274 at 300 MHz
					0.398 at 600 MHz
					0.527 at 1 GHz
URM90	1/0.6 mm	6	75	67	1.12 at 100 MHz
					3.91 at 1GHz
URM95	1/0.46 mm	2.3	50	100	0.27 at 100 MHz
					0.37 at 200 MHz
					0.46 at 300 MHz
					0.65 at 600 MHz
URM96	1/0.64 mm	6	95	40	0.79 at 100 MHz
					2.58 at 1 GHz
URM202	7/0.25 mm	5.1	75	56	0.086 at 60 MHz
					0.11 at 100 MHz
					0.16 at 200 MHz
					0.27 at 500 MHz
					0.4 at 900 MHz
URM203	1/1.12 mm	7.25	75	56	0.057 at 60 MHz
					0.075 at 100 MHz
					0.11 at 200 MHz
					0.185 at 500 MHz
					0.26 at 900 MHz
2001	7/0.2 mm	4.6	75	56.7	0.04 at 5 MHZ
					0.14 at 60 MHz
					0.253 at 200 MHz
2002	7/0.2 mm	5.2	75	56.7	0.0126 at 1 MHz
					0.042 at 10 MHz
					0.138 at 100 MHz
2003A	7/0.2 mm	6.9	75	67	0.026 at 5 MHz
					0.09 at 60 MHz
					0.185 at 200 MHz
Ethernet trunk cable	1/2.17 mm	10.3	50	85	0.02 at 5 MHz
					0.04 at 10 MHz

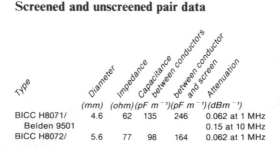

Screened and unscreened pair data

Type	Diameter (mm)	Impedance (ohm)	Capacitance between conductors (pF m⁻¹)	between conductor and screen (pF m⁻¹)	Attenuation (dBm⁻¹)
BICC H8071/ Belden 9501	4.6	62	135	246	0.062 at 1 MHz
					0.15 at 10 MHz
BICC H8072/	5.6	77	98	164	0.062 at 1 MHz

Type	Diameter (mm)	Impedance (ohm)	Capacitance between conductors (pF m⁻¹)	between conductor and screen (pF m⁻¹)	Attenuation (dBm⁻¹)
Belden 9502 (2 pair)					0.15 at 10 MHz
BICC H8073/ Belden 9504 (4 pair)	6.7	77	98	154	0.062 at 1 MHz 0.15 at 10 MHz
BICC H8074/ Belden 9506 (6 pair)	7.6	77	98	164	0.062 at 1 MHz 0.15 at 10 MHz
H8082/Belden 8761	5.4	85	79	154	
BICC H8085/ Belden 8723 (2 pair)	4.19	54	115	203	
BICC H8086/ Belden 8777 (3 pair)	7.9	62	98	180	
BICC H8088/ Belden 8774 (9 pair)	11.9	62	98	180	
BICC H8150/ Belden 8795	4.0	110	56	n/a	0.016 at 1 MHz 0.063 at 10 MHz
Belden 8205/ Alpha 1895	4.8		55	n/a	
Belden 8761	4.6	85	79	154	
Belden 9855/ Alpha 9819	7.7	108	46		0.02 at 1 MHz
Belden 9891 (4 pair)	10.03	78	64.6	113.8	
Belden 9892 (4 pair)	10.67	78	64.6	113.8	
Belden 9893 (5 pair)	12.95	78	64.6	113.8	

Note:
n/a = not applicable (unscreened cable)

Cable equivalents

Alpha	Belden	BICC	Brand Rex	Notes
1895	8205			Unscreened pair
	8216	T3390		
	8259	T3429		
2401	8761	H8082	BE-56761	
	8262	T3428		
	8263	T3429		
2461	8451	H8084	BI-56451	

Alpha	Belden	BICC	Brand Rex	Notes
2466	8723	H8085	BI-56723	2-pair, 58 ohm, UL2493
2401	8761	H8082		UL2092
2403	8771	H8101		UL2093
6022	8773	H8118	BE-56773	27-pair 55 ohm, UL2919
6014	8774	H8088	BE-56774	9-pair 55 ohm, UL2493
6010	8777	H8086	BE-56777	3-pair 55 ohm, UL2493
1202	8795	H8105		Unscreened-pair 110 ohm
	9204	T3429		
9817	9207	H8106	BC-57207	IBM7362211, UL2498
9818	9207	H8106	BC-57207	IBM7362211, UL2498
9063	9269	T3430		RG62A/U, UL1478
9815	9272	H8065	BC-57272	Twin-axial 78 ohm, UL2092
5902	9302	H8079	BE-57302	
5471	9501	H8071		1-pair 62 ohm, UL2464
5472	9502	H8072	BE-57502	2-pair 77 ohm, UL2464
5473	9503	H8136	BE-57503	3-pair 77 ohm, UL2464
5474	9504	H8073	BE-57504	4-pair 77 ohm, UL2464
5475	9505	H8173	BE-57505	5-pair 77 ohm, UL2464
5476	9506	H8074	BE-57506	6-pair 77 ohm, UL2464
5480	9510	H8133	BE-57510	10-pair 85 ohm, UL2464
5480	9515	H8076	BE-57515	15-pair 95 ohm, UL2464
9845	9555	H8119	BC-57555	RG59B/U, Wang 420-0057
	9696	H8064		
	9729	H9002	BE-57555	UL2493
6017	9768	H8113	BE-57768	12-pair 55 ohm, UL2493
	9829	H9564		UL2919
9819	9855	H8063		UL2919, UL2582
	9880	H8112	BC-57880	Ethernet trunk coaxial
	9881			Multicore + coax, UL2704
	9892		BN-57892	Ethernet, 4-pair
		2002		ICL80047293, UL1354
		H9601	GT-75340	ICL80049808
			GT-553011	ICL80048808, Oslan
			GT-551014	ICL80049496, Cheapernet

Important note:
Cable types listed above may not be *exact* equivalents. Readers are advised to consult manufacturers' data before ordering.

Recommended cables

Application	Type	Recommended cable
Cheapernet	Coax	Brand Rex GT551014, ICL 80049496
Data communications in noisy environments	Twin-axial	Alpha 9817, Belden 9207, IBM 7362211
Data communications, low cross-talk	Multipair	Belden 8723, 8777, 8774 etc.

Application	Type	Recommended cable
Ethernet trunk	Coax	Belden 9880, BICC 8112, NEK 06214
Ethernet drop	4-pair, plus drain	Belden 9892, Brand Rex BN-57892, NEK 06668
General-purpose	1-pair (unscreened)	Alpha 1202, Belden 8795, BICC H8150
General-purpose	Multi-pair	Belden 9502, 9504, 9506 etc.
General-purpose	RG62A/U coax	Alpha 9062A, Belden 9269, BICC T3430
General-purpose data/ control	Multicore plus coax	Belden 9881
HF radio	URM43 coax	Uniradio M43
Oslan drop	4-pair, plus drain	BICC H960, Brand Rex GT553011, ICL 80048808
Point-of-sale terminals	2-pair	Alpha 9819, Belden 9855, BICC H8063, IBM 1657265
VHF/UHF radio	URM67 coax	Uniradio M67 (equivalent to RG213/U)

Important note:
Readers are advised to consult manufacturer's data in order to check the suitability of cables before ordering.

Optical fibre technology

Optical fibres are becoming widely used as a transmission medium for long-haul data communications and in local area networks (LAN). It is now possible to obtain data rates in excess of 4 Gbps over distances of greater than 100 km and 140 Mbps at distances over 220 km.

Optical fibres offer some very significant advantages over conventional waveguides and coaxial cables. These can be summarised as follows:

- Optical cables are lightweight and of small physical size
- Exceptional bandwidths are available within the medium
- Relative freedom from electromagnetic interference
- Significantly reduced noise and cross-talk compared with conventional data cables
- Relatively low values of attenuation within the medium
- High reliability coupled with long operational life
- Electrical isolation and freedom from earth/ground loops
- Very high security of transmission

Optical fibres and their associated high-speed optical sources and detectors are particularly well suited to the transmission of wideband digitally encoded information. This permits the medium to be used for high-speed data communications, local and wide area networking applications

Propagation
Essentially, an optical fibre consists of a cylindrical glass core surrounded by glass cladding. The fibre acts as a dielectric waveguide in which the electromagnetic wave (of appropriate frequency) will propagate with minimal loss.

Refraction towards the normal

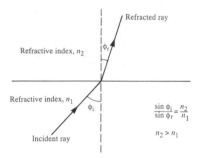

Refracted ray

Refractive index, n_2 ϕ_r

Refractive index, n_1 ϕ_i

$$\frac{\sin \phi_i}{\sin \phi_r} = \frac{n_2}{n_1}$$

$$n_2 > n_1$$

Incident ray

Refraction away from the normal

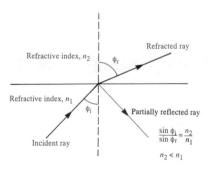

Refracted ray

Refractive index, n_2 ϕ_r

Refractive index, n_1

ϕ_i Partially reflected ray

$$\frac{\sin \phi_i}{\sin \phi_r} = \frac{n_2}{n_1}$$

$$n_2 < n_1$$

Incident ray

Much of fibre optics is governed by the fundamental laws of refraction. When a light wave passes from a medium of higher refractive index to one of lower refractive index, the wave is bent towards the normal. Conversely, when travelling from a medium of lower refractive index to one of higher refractive index, the wave will be bent away from the normal. In this latter case, some of the incident light will be reflected at the boundary of the two media and, as the angle of incidence is increased, the angle of refraction will also be increased until, at a critical value, the light wave will be totally reflected (ie, the refracted ray will no longer exist). The angle of incidence at which this occurs is known as the critical angle, ϕ_c. The value of ϕ_c depends upon the absolute refractive indices of the media and is given by:

$$\phi_c = \sqrt{\frac{2(n_1 - n_2)}{n_1}}$$

where n_1 and n_2 are the refractive indices of the more dense and less dense media respectively.

Optical fibres are drawn from the molten state and are thus of cylindrical construction. The more dense medium is surrounded by the less dense cladding. Provided the angle of incidence of the input wave is larger than the critical angle, the light wave will propagate along the fibre by means of a series of total reflections. Any other light waves that are incident on the upper boundary at an angle $\phi > \phi_c$ will also propagate along the inner medium. Conversely, any light wave that is incident upon the upper boundary with $\phi <_c$ will pass into the outer medium and will be lost there by scattering and/or absorption.

Launching

Having briefly considered propagation within the fibre, we shall turn our attention to the mechanism by which waves are launched. The cone of acceptance is defined as the complete set of angles which will be subject to total internal reflection. Rays entering from the edges will take a longer path through the fibre but will travel faster because of the lower refractive index of the outer layer. The numerical aperture determines the bandwidth of the fibre and is given by:

$$NA = \sin \phi_a$$

Clearly, when a number of light waves enter the system with differing angles of incidence, a number of waves (or modes) are able to propagate. This multimode propagation is relatively simple to achieve but has the attendant disadvantage that, since the light waves will take different times to pass through the fibre, the variation of transit time will result in dispersion, which imposes an obvious restriction on the maximum bit rate that the system will support.

The cone of acceptance

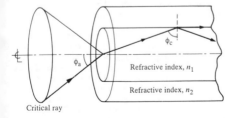

Critical ray

Total internal reflection

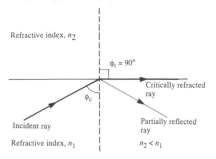

Multimode propagation

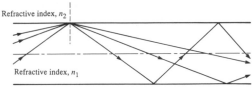

There are two methods for minimising multimode propagation. One uses a fibre of graded refractive index, while the other uses a special monomode fibre. The inner core of this type of fibre is reduced in diameter so that it is of the same order of magnitude as the wavelength of the incident wave. This ensures that only one mode will successfully propagate.

Attenuation

The loss within an optical fibre arises from a number of causes including: absorption, scattering in the core (due to non-homogeneity of the refractive index), scattering at the core/cladding boundary, and losses due to radiation at bends in the fibre.

The attenuation coefficient of an optical fibre refers only to losses in the fibre itself and neglects coupling and bending losses. In general, the attenuation of a good quality fibre can be expected to be approximately $1\,\mathrm{dB\,km^{-1}}$ at a wavelength of 1300 nm. Hence a 5 km length of fibre can be expected to exhibit a loss of around 5 dB (excluding losses due to coupling and bending).

Whereas the attenuation coefficient of an optical fibre is largely dependent upon the quality and consistency of the glass used for the core and cladding, the attenuation of all optical fibres varies widely with wavelength. The typical attenuation/wavelength characteristic for a monomode fibre is shown in the figure below. It should be noted that the sharp peak at about $1.39\,\mu m$ arises from excess absorption within the monomode fibre.

Typical attenuation/wavelength characteristic for a monomode optical fibre

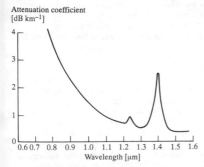

Monomode fibres are now a common feature of high-speed data communication systems and manufacturing techniques have been developed which ensure consistent and reliable products with low attenuation and wide operational bandwidths. However, since monomode fibres are significantly smaller in diameter than their multimode predecessors, a consistent and reliable means of cutting, surface preparation, alignment and interconnection is essential.

Relative dimensions of multimode and monomode fibres

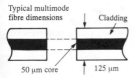

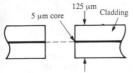

Optical fibre connectors

The essential requirements for optical fibre connectors are:

- Low cost
- Robustness
- Repeatability (over numerous mating operations)
- Reliability
- Suitability for installation 'in the field'
- Low loss

Whilst the loss exhibited by a connector may be quoted in absolute terms, it is often specified in terms of an equivalent length of optical fibre. This technique is particularly relevant in the appraisal of long-haul networks. If, for example, two connectors are used at a repeater, the overall connector loss may approach 4 dB. This is equivalent to several kilometres of low-loss fibre! If the connector loss can be reduced, then the spacing between repeaters can be increased and the overall number of repeaters can be reduced accordingly.

While optical fibres are ideal for use in long-haul and wideband networking applications, they are also suitable for low-speed local applications where high security and/or reliability of data transfer is required or where a very high noise level would preclude the use of conventional cables. A fibre optic RS-232 interface is available from several manufacturers. This device is fitted with standard SMA connectors for use with 50/125 μm or 200 μm optical cables which operate at a wavelength of 820 nm. SMA terminated optical cables having lengths of between 2 m and 500 m are available from several suppliers.

For very short distance applications, inexpensive polymer fibres may be used. These fibres are generally designed for use at wavelengths of around 665 nm (visible red light); however, since they generally exhibit attenuation of around 200 dB km^{-1}, they are only suitable for short distances (ie, typically less than 50 m).

Optical sources

Suitably mounted and encapsulated light emitting diodes (LED) and laser diodes (LD) are commonly used as sources in conjunction with optical fibres. The following table summarises the typical characteristics of these optical sources:

Device type	Material	Operating wavelength (nm)	Bit rate (Mbps)	Transmission range (km)
LED	AlGaAs	850	0 to 40	0 to 5
LED	InGaAsP	1300	0 to 300	5 to 10
LD	InGaAsP	1300	30 to 800	10 to 50
LD	InGaAsP	1550	100 to 800	50 to 100

Optical detectors

Appropriately mounted and encapsulated photodiodes (PD) or avalanche photodiodes (APD) are commonly used as detectors in conjunction with optical fibres. The following table summarises the typical characteristics of these optical detectors:

Device type	Material	Operating wavelength (nm)	Bit rate (Mbps)	Transmission range (km)
PD	Si	850	0 to 30	0 to 2
APD	Si	850	0 to 40	2 to 5
APD	InGaAs	1300	0 to 300	5 to 50
APD	InGaAs	1550	100 to 800	50 to 100

PC Video display modes and adapter standards

Mode	Display type	Colours	Screen resolution (note 1)	MDA	CGA	EGA	MCGA	VGA	HGA (note 3)
00H	Text	16	40 × 25		*	*	*	*	*
01H	Text	16	40 × 25		*	*	*	*	
02H	Text	16	80 × 25		*	*	*	*	
03H	Text	16	80 × 25		*	*	*	*	
04H	Graphics	4	320 × 200		*	*	*	*	
05H	Graphics	4	320 × 200		*	*	*	*	
06H	Graphics	2	640 × 200		*	*	*	*	
07H	Text	Mono	80 × 25	*		*		*	*
08H	Graphics	16	160 × 200	(note 2)					
09H	Graphics	16	320 × 200	(note 2)					
0AH	Graphics	4	640 × 200	(note 2)					
0BH	(note 4)								
0CH	(note 4)								
0DH	Graphics	16	320 × 200			*		*	
0EH	Graphics	16	640 × 200			*		*	
0FH	Graphics	Mono	640 × 350			*		*	
10H	Graphics	16	640 × 350			*		*	
11H	Graphics	2	640 × 480				*	*	
12H	Graphics	16	640 × 480					*	
13H	Graphics	256	320 × 200				*	*	

Notes:

1 Resolutions are quoted in (columns × lines) for text displays and (horizontal × vertical) pixels for graphics displays.

2 Applies only to the PCjr.

3 The Hercules Graphics Adapter card successfully combines the graphics (but NOT colour) capabilities of the CGA adapter with the high quality text display of the MDA adapter.

4 Reserved mode.

Transmission element specifications

The transmission path in a data communications system may comprise cables, amplifiers/regenerators, attenuators, filters, diplexers etc. The electrical characteristics of such items are usually specified in terms of one, or more of the following parameters.

Gain or loss

The gain or loss of an element within a transmission path is the ratio of output voltage to input voltage (ie, voltage gain), output current to input current (ie, current gain), or output power to input power (ie, power gain). Gain is often expressed in decibels (dB) where:

$$\text{voltage gain in dB} = 20 \log_{10}\left(\frac{\text{Vout}}{\text{Vin}}\right)$$

$$\text{current gain in dB} = 20 \log_{10}\left(\frac{\text{Iout}}{\text{Iin}}\right)$$

$$\text{power gain in dB} = 10 \log_{10}\left(\frac{\text{Pout}}{\text{Pin}}\right)$$

Note that in the two former cases, the specification is only meaningful where the input and output impedances of the element are identical

Input impedance

The input impedance of an element within a transmission path is the ratio of input voltage to input current and it is expressed in ohms. The input of an amplifier is normally purely resistive (ie, the reactive component is negligible) in the middle of its working frequency range (ie, the mid-band) and hence, in such cases, input impedance is synonymous with input resistance.

Output impedance

The output impedance of an element within a transmission path is the ratio of open-circuit output voltage to short-circuit output current and is measured in ohms. Note that this impedance is internal to the element and should not be confused with the impedance of the load or circuit to which the element is connected. (Usually, but not always, these will have identical values in order to maximise power transfer).

Frequency response

The frequency response of a transmission element is usually specified in terms of the upper and lower cut-off frequencies of the element. These frequencies are those at which the output power has dropped to 50% (otherwise known as the -3dB points) or where the voltage gain has dropped to 70.7% of its mid-band value.

Bandwidth

The bandwidth of a transmission element is usually taken as the difference between the two cut-off frequencies. It is equivalent to the frequency span for which the gain is maintained within defined limits (usually within 3dB of the mid-band power gain).

Phase shift

The phase shift of a transmission element is defined as the phase angle (in electrical degrees or radians) of the output signal when compared with the input signal (taken as the reference). Phase shift is substantially constant within the mid-band region but is liable to a marked variation beyond cut-off due to the increasing significance of reactance.

Equivalent circuit of a transmission element

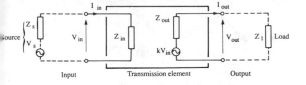

Frequency response of a transmission element

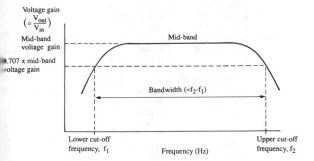

Decibels and ratios of power, voltage and current

dB	Power ratio	Voltage/current ratio
−99	1.258925×10^{-10}	1.122018×10^{-5}
−98	1.584893×10^{-10}	1.258925×10^{-5}
−97	1.995262×10^{-10}	1.412538×10^{-5}
−96	2.511887×10^{-10}	1.584893×10^{-5}
−95	3.162278×10^{-10}	1.778279×10^{-5}
−94	3.981072×10^{-10}	1.995262×10^{-5}
−93	5.011873×10^{-10}	2.238721×10^{-5}
−92	6.309573×10^{-10}	2.511886×10^{-5}
−91	7.943282×10^{-10}	2.818383×10^{-5}
−90	$\mathbf{1 \times 10^{-9}}$	$\mathbf{3.162278 \times 10^{-5}}$
−89	1.258925×10^{-9}	3.548134×10^{-5}
−88	1.584893×10^{-9}	3.981072×10^{-5}
−87	1.995262×10^{-9}	4.466836×10^{-5}
−86	2.511886×10^{-9}	5.011872×10^{-5}
−85	3.162278×10^{-9}	5.623413×10^{-5}
−84	3.981072×10^{-9}	6.309574×10^{-5}
−83	5.011872×10^{-9}	7.079458×10^{-5}

dB	Power ratio	Voltage/current ratio
−82	6.309573×10^{-9}	7.943282×10^{-5}
−81	7.943282×10^{-9}	8.91251×10^{-5}
−80	1×10^{-8}	1×10^{-4}
−79	1.258925×10^{-8}	1.122018×10^{-4}
−78	1.584893×10^{-8}	1.258925×10^{-4}
−77	1.995262×10^{-8}	1.412538×10^{-4}
−76	2.511887×10^{-8}	1.584893×10^{-4}
−75	3.162278×10^{-8}	1.778279×10^{-4}
−74	3.981072×10^{-8}	1.995262×10^{-4}
−73	5.011873×10^{-8}	2.238721×10^{-4}
−72	6.309573×10^{-8}	2.511886×10^{-4}
−71	7.943282×10^{-8}	2.818383×10^{-4}
−70	1×10^{-7}	3.162278×10^{-4}
−69	1.258925×10^{-7}	3.548134×10^{-4}
−68	1.584893×10^{-7}	3.981072×10^{-4}
−67	1.995262×10^{-7}	4.466836×10^{-4}
−66	2.511887×10^{-7}	5.011872×10^{-4}
−65	3.162278×10^{-7}	5.623413×10^{-4}
−64	3.981072×10^{-7}	6.309574×10^{-4}
−63	5.011872×10^{-7}	7.079458×10^{-4}
−62	6.309573×10^{-7}	7.943282×10^{-4}
−61	7.943282×10^{-7}	8.91251×10^{-4}
−60	1×10^{-6}	1×10^{-3}
−59	1.258925×10^{-6}	1.122018×10^{-3}
−58	1.584893×10^{-6}	1.258925×10^{-3}
−57	1.995262×10^{-6}	1.412538×10^{-3}
−56	2.511886×10^{-6}	1.584893×10^{-3}
−55	3.162278×10^{-6}	1.778279×10^{-3}
−54	3.981072×10^{-6}	1.995262×10^{-3}
−53	5.011872×10^{-6}	2.238721×10^{-3}
−52	6.309574×10^{-6}	2.511886×10^{-3}
−51	7.943282×10^{-6}	2.818383×10^{-3}
−50	1×10^{-5}	3.162278×10^{-3}
−49	1.258925×10^{-5}	3.548134×10^{-3}
−48	1.584893×10^{-5}	3.981072×10^{-3}
−47	1.995262×10^{-5}	4.466836×10^{-3}
−46	2.511886×10^{-5}	5.011872×10^{-3}
−45	3.162278×10^{-5}	5.623413×10^{-3}
−44	3.981072×10^{-5}	6.309574×10^{-3}
−43	5.011872×10^{-5}	7.079458×10^{-3}
−42	6.309574×10^{-5}	7.943282×10^{-3}
−41	7.943282×10^{-5}	8.912509×10^{-3}
−40	1×10^{-4}	**0.01**
−39	1.258925×10^{-4}	0.01122018
−38	1.584893×10^{-4}	0.01258925
−37	1.995262×10^{-4}	0.01412538
−36	2.511886×10^{-4}	0.01584893
−35	3.162278×10^{-4}	0.01778279
−34	3.981072×10^{-4}	0.01995262
−33	5.011872×10^{-4}	0.02238721
−32	6.309574×10^{-4}	0.02511887
−31	7.943282×10^{-4}	0.02818383

dB	Power ratio	Voltage/current ratio
-30	**1 × 10⁻³**	**0.03162277**
-29	1.258925 × 10⁻³	0.03548134
-28	1.584893 × 10⁻³	0.03981072
-27	1.995262 × 10⁻³	0.04466836
-26	2.511886 × 10⁻³	0.05011872
-25	3.162278 × 10⁻³	0.05623413
-24	3.981072 × 10⁻³	0.06309573
-23	5.011872 × 10⁻³	0.07079457
-22	6.309574 × 10⁻³	0.07943282
-21	7.943282 × 10⁻³	0.0891251
-20	**0.01**	**0.1**
-19	0.01258925	0.1122018
-18	0.01584893	0.1258925
-17	0.01995262	0.1412538
-16	0.02511887	0.1584893
-15	0.03162277	0.1778279
-14	0.03981072	0.1995262
-13	0.05011872	0.2238721
-12	0.06309573	0.2511886
-11	0.07943282	0.2818383
-10	**0.1**	**0.3162278**
-9	0.1258925	0.3548134
-8	0.1584893	0.3981072
-7	0.1995262	0.4466836
-6	0.2511886	0.5011872
-5	0.3162278	0.5623413
-4	0.3981072	0.6309574
-3	0.5011872	0.7079458
-2	0.6309574	0.7943282
-1	0.7943282	0.891251
-0	**1**	**1**
1	1.258925	1.122018
2	1.584893	1.258925
3	1.995262	1.412538
4	2.511886	1.584893
5	3.162278	1.778279
6	3.981072	1.995262
7	5.011872	2.238721
8	6.309574	2.511886
9	7.943282	2.818383
10	**10**	**3.162278**
11	12.58925	3.548134
12	15.84893	3.981072
13	19.95262	4.466836
14	25.11886	5.011872
15	31.62278	5.623413
16	39.81072	6.309574
17	50.11872	7.079458
18	63.09573	7.943282
19	79.43282	8.912509
20	**100**	**10**
21	125.8925	11.22018

dB	Power ratio	Voltage/current ratio
22	158.4893	12.58925
23	199.5262	14.12538
24	251.1886	15.84893
25	316.2278	17.78279
26	398.1072	19.95262
27	501.1872	22.38721
28	630.9573	25.11886
29	794.3282	28.18383
30	**1000**	**31.62278**
31	1258.925	35.48134
32	1584.893	39.81072
33	1995.262	44.66836
34	2511.886	50.11872
35	3162.278	56.23413
36	3981.072	63.09573
37	5011.873	70.79458
38	6309.573	79.43282
39	7943.282	89.12509
40	**10000**	**100**
41	12589.25	112.2018
42	15848.93	125.8925
43	19952.62	141.2538
44	25118.86	158.4893
45	31622.78	177.8279
46	39810.72	199.5262
47	50118.72	223.8721
48	63095.73	251.1886
49	79432.82	281.8383
50	**100000**	**316.2278**
51	125892.5	354.8134
52	158489.3	398.1072
53	199526.2	446.6836
54	251188.6	501.1872
55	316227.8	562.3413
56	398107.2	630.9573
57	501187.2	707.9458
58	630957.3	794.3282
59	794328.2	891.2509
60	**1000000**	**1000**
61	1258925	1122.018
62	1584893	1258.925
63	1995262	1412.538
64	2511886	1584.893
65	3162278	1778.279
66	3981072	1995.262
67	5011872	2238.721
68	6309573	2511.886
69	7943282	2818.383
70	**1×10^7**	**3162.278**
71	1.258925×10^7	3548.134
72	1.584893×10^7	3981.072
73	1.995262×10^7	4466.836

dB	Power ratio	Voltage/current ratio
74	2.511886×10^7	5011.872
75	3.162278×10^7	5623.413
76	3.981072×10^7	6309.573
77	5.011872×10^7	7079.458
78	6.309574×10^7	7943.282
79	7.943282×10^7	8912.51
80	$\mathbf{1 \times 10^8}$	**10000**
81	1.258925×10^8	11220.18
82	1.584893×10^8	12589.25
83	1.995262×10^8	14125.37
84	2.511886×10^8	15848.93
85	3.162278×10^8	17782.79
86	3.981072×10^8	19952.62
87	5.011872×10^8	22387.21
88	6.309573×10^8	25118.86
89	7.943283×10^8	28183.83
90	$\mathbf{1 \times 10^9}$	**31622.78**
91	1.258925×10^9	35481.34
92	1.584893×10^9	39810.72
93	1.995262×10^9	44668.36
94	2.511886×10^9	50118.72
95	3.162278×10^9	56234.13
96	3.981072×10^9	63095.73
97	5.011872×10^9	70794.58
98	6.309574×10^9	79432.82
99	7.943282×10^9	89125.09
100	$\mathbf{1 \times 10^{10}}$	**100000**

Transmission line power levels and voltages

Level (dBm)	Power (W)	Line voltage (V)	
		$Z_o = 50 ohm$	$Z_o = 75 ohm$
−39	1.258×10^{-7}	2.508×10^{-3}	3.072×10^{-3}
−38	1.584×10^{-7}	2.815×10^{-3}	3.447×10^{-3}
−37	1.995×10^{-7}	3.158×10^{-3}	3.868×10^{-3}
−36	2.511×10^{-7}	3.543×10^{-3}	4.340×10^{-3}
−35	3.162×10^{-7}	3.976×10^{-3}	4.870×10^{-3}
−34	3.981×10^{-7}	4.461×10^{-3}	5.464×10^{-3}
−33	5.011×10^{-7}	5.005×10^{-3}	6.130×10^{-3}
−32	6.309×10^{-7}	5.616×10^{-3}	6.879×10^{-3}
−31	7.943×10^{-7}	6.302×10^{-3}	7.718×10^{-3}
−30	$\mathbf{1.000 \times 10^{-6}}$	$\mathbf{7.071 \times 10^{-3}}$	$\mathbf{8.660 \times 10^{-3}}$
−29	1.258×10^{-6}	7.933×10^{-3}	9.716×10^{-3}
−28	1.584×10^{-6}	8.901×10^{-3}	1.090×10^{-2}
−27	1.995×10^{-6}	9.988×10^{-3}	1.223×10^{-2}

Level (dBm)	Power (W)	Line voltage (V) $Z_o=50\,ohm$	$Z_o=75\,ohm$
−26	2.511×10^{-6}	1.120×10^{-2}	1.372×10^{-2}
−25	3.162×10^{-6}	1.257×10^{-2}	1.540×10^{-2}
−24	3.981×10^{-6}	1.410×10^{-2}	1.727×10^{-2}
−23	5.011×10^{-6}	1.583×10^{-2}	1.938×10^{-2}
−22	6.309×10^{-6}	1.776×10^{-2}	2.175×10^{-2}
−21	7.943×10^{-6}	1.992×10^{-2}	2.440×10^{-2}
−20	$\mathbf{9.999 \times 10^{-6}}$	$\mathbf{2.236 \times 10^{-2}}$	$\mathbf{2.738 \times 10^{-2}}$
−19	1.258×10^{-5}	2.508×10^{-2}	3.072×10^{-2}
−18	1.584×10^{-5}	2.815×10^{-2}	3.447×10^{-2}
−17	1.995×10^{-5}	3.158×10^{-2}	3.868×10^{-2}
−16	2.511×10^{-5}	3.543×10^{-2}	4.340×10^{-2}
−15	3.162×10^{-5}	3.976×10^{-2}	4.870×10^{-2}
−14	3.981×10^{-5}	4.461×10^{-2}	5.464×10^{-2}
−13	5.011×10^{-5}	5.005×10^{-2}	6.130×10^{-2}
−12	6.309×10^{-5}	5.616×10^{-2}	6.879×10^{-2}
−11	7.943×10^{-5}	6.302×10^{-2}	7.718×10^{-2}
−10	$\mathbf{9.999 \times 10^{-5}}$	$\mathbf{7.071 \times 10^{-2}}$	$\mathbf{8.660 \times 10^{-2}}$
−9	1.258×10^{-4}	7.933×10^{-2}	9.716×10^{-2}
−8	1.584×10^{-4}	8.901×10^{-2}	1.090×10^{-1}
−7	1.995×10^{-4}	9.988×10^{-2}	1.223×10^{-1}
−6	2.511×10^{-4}	1.120×10^{-1}	1.372×10^{-1}
−5	3.162×10^{-4}	1.257×10^{-1}	1.540×10^{-1}
−4	3.981×10^{-4}	1.410×10^{-1}	1.727×10^{-1}
−3	5.011×10^{-4}	1.583×10^{-1}	1.938×10^{-1}
−2	6.309×10^{-4}	1.776×10^{-1}	2.175×10^{-1}
−1	7.943×10^{-4}	1.992×10^{-1}	2.440×10^{-1}
−0	$\mathbf{1.000 \times 10^{-3}}$	$\mathbf{2.236 \times 10^{-1}}$	$\mathbf{2.738 \times 10^{-1}}$
1	1.258×10^{-3}	2.508×10^{-1}	3.072×10^{-1}
2	1.584×10^{-3}	2.815×10^{-1}	3.447×10^{-1}
3	1.995×10^{-3}	3.158×10^{-1}	3.868×10^{-1}
4	2.511×10^{-3}	3.543×10^{-1}	4.340×10^{-1}
5	3.162×10^{-3}	3.976×10^{-1}	4.870×10^{-1}
6	3.981×10^{-3}	4.461×10^{-1}	5.464×10^{-1}
7	5.011×10^{-3}	5.005×10^{-1}	6.130×10^{-1}
8	6.309×10^{-3}	5.616×10^{-1}	6.879×10^{-1}
9	7.943×10^{-3}	6.302×10^{-1}	7.718×10^{-1}
10	$\mathbf{9.999 \times 10^{-3}}$	$\mathbf{7.071 \times 10^{-1}}$	$\mathbf{8.660 \times 10^{-1}}$
11	1.258×10^{-2}	7.933×10^{-1}	9.716×10^{-1}
12	1.584×10^{-2}	8.901×10^{-1}	1.090
13	1.995×10^{-2}	9.988×10^{-1}	1.223
14	2.511×10^{-2}	1.120	1.372
15	3.162×10^{-2}	1.257	1.540
16	3.981×10^{-2}	1.410	1.727
17	5.011×10^{-2}	1.583	1.938
18	6.309×10^{-2}	1.776	2.175
19	7.943×10^{-2}	1.992	2.440
20	$\mathbf{1.000 \times 10^{-1}}$	**2.236**	**2.738**
21	1.258×10^{-1}	2.508	3.072
22	1.584×10^{-1}	2.815	3.447
23	1.995×10^{-1}	3.158	3.868
24	2.511×10^{-1}	3.543	4.340
25	3.162×10^{-1}	3.976	4.870

Level (dBm)	Power (W)	Line voltage (V)	
		$Z_o = 50\,ohm$	$Z_o = 75\,ohm$
26	3.981×10^{-1}	4.461	5.464
27	5.011×10^{-1}	5.005	6.130
28	6.309×10^{-1}	5.616	6.879
29	7.943×10^{-1}	6.302	7.718
30	**1.000**	**7.071**	**8.660**
31	1.258	7.933	9.716
32	1.584	8.901	1.090×10^1
33	1.995	9.988	1.223×10^1
34	2.511	1.120×10^1	1.372×10^1
35	3.162	1.257×10^1	1.540×10^1
36	3.981	1.410×10^1	1.727×10^1
37	5.011	1.583×10^1	1.938×10^1
38	6.309	1.776×10^1	2.175×10^1
39	7.943	1.992×10^1	2.440×10^1
40	$\mathbf{1.000 \times 10^{-1}}$	$\mathbf{2.236 \times 10^1}$	$\mathbf{2.738 \times 10^1}$

Flowchart symbols

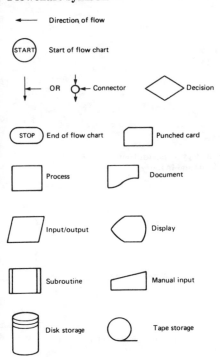

- ← Direction of flow
- (START) Start of flow chart
- ↓ OR ○ ← Connector
- ◇ Decision
- (STOP) End of flow chart
- Punched card
- Process
- Document
- Input/output
- Display
- Subroutine
- Manual input
- Disk storage
- Tape storage

Addresses of advisory bodies, standards institutes, and other organisations

American National Standards Institute (ANSI)
1430 Broadway
New York
NU 10018

British Standards Institute (BS)
Linford Wood
Milton Keynes
MK14 6LE

CCITT
Place due Nations
CH-1211 Geneva 20
Switzerland

Electronic Industries Association (EIA)
Engineering Department
2001 Eye Street
Washington DC 20006

European Computer Manufacturers Association (ECMA)
114 Rue de Rhone
CH-1204 Geneva
Switzerland

IEEE Computer Society
1109 Spring Street
Suite 300
Silver Spring
MD 20910

IEEE Standards Board
345 East 47th Street
New York 10017

Information Technology Standards Unit
Department of Trade and Industry
29 Bressenden Place
London
SW1E 5DT

Institute of Electrical Engineers (IEE)
Savoy Place
London
WC2R 0BL

International Standards Organisation (ISO)
1 Rue de Varembe
CH-1211
Geneva
Switzerland

International Telecommunications Union (ITU)
Place des Nations
1121 Geneva 2
Switzerland

National Bureau of Standards (NBS)
Technical Information and Publications Division
Washington DC 20234

National Computing Centre (NCC)
Oxford Road
Manchester
M1 7ED

US Department of Commerce
National Technical Information Service
5285 Port Royal Road
Springfield
VA 22161

Glossary of data communications terms

Acknowledgment A signal which indicates that data has been received without error.

Acoustic coupler A device which allows a modem to be connected to a conventional telephone handset. Signals are fed to and from the handset in the form of audible tones and hence there is no need for a hardwired connection to the line.

Address A reference to the location of the source or destination of data. Each node within a network must be given a unique numeric identifying address.

Alternating mode Half-duplex (ie, alternate send/receive) operation.

Amplifier Circuit or device which increases the power of an electrical signal.

Amplitude Peak excursion of a signal from its rest or mean value (usually specified in volts).

Amplitude modulation A modulation method in which the amplitude of a carrier is modified in accordance with the transmitted information.

Analog transmission Method of transmission in which information is conveyed by analog (eg, sinusoidal) signals.

Application layer The top layer of the ISO model for OSI.

Asynchronous transmission Transmission method in which the time between transmitted characters is arbitrary. Transmission is controlled by *start* and *stop* bits and no additional synchronising or timing information is required.

Attenuation Decrease in the magnitude of a signal (in terms of power, voltage or current) in a circuit.

Balanced In an *electrical* context a balanced line is one in which differential signals are employed (ie, neither of the conducting paths is returned to earth). In the context of the *data link layer* a balanced protocol is one involving a peer relationship of equal status (ie, not master-slave).

Band splitter A multiplexer which divides the available bandwidth into several independent sub-channels of reduced bandwidth (and consequently reduced data rate when compared with the original channel).

Bandwidth Range of frequencies occupied by a signal or available within a communication channel. Bandwidth is normally specified within certain defined limits and can be considered to be the difference between the upper (maximum) and lower (minimum) frequencies within the channel.

Baseband The range of frequencies occupied by a digital signal (unchanged by modulation) which typically extends from d.c. to several tens or hundreds of kilohertz depending upon the data rate employed.

Baseband LAN A local area network which employs baseband transmission techniques.

Baseband transmission Transmission method in which digital signals are passed, without modulation, directly through the transmission medium.

Baud A unit of signalling speed expressed in terms of the number of signal events per second.

Baud rate Signalling rate (note that this is not necessarily the same as the number of bits transmitted per second).

Baudot code A code used for data transmission in which each character is represented by five bits. Shift characters are used so that a full set of upper and lower case letters, figures and punctuation can be transmitted.

Binary synchronous communication IBM communication protocol which employs a defined set of control characters and control sequences for synchronised transmission of binary coded data (often referred to as *bisync*).

Bit A contraction of 'binary digit'; a single digit in a binary number.

Bit rate The rate at which bits are transmitted expressed in *bits per second* (bps)

Block A contiguous sequence of data characters transmited as one unit. Additional characters or codes may be added to the block to permit flow control (eg, synchronisation and error detection).

Block check character A character tagged to the end of a block which provides a means of verifying that the block has been received without error. The character is derived from a pre-defined algorithm.

Blocking In the context of *PBX*, blocking refers to an inability to provide a connection path. In the context of the *data link layer* of the ISO model for OSI, blocking refers to the combination of several blocks into one frame.

Break A request to terminate transmission.

Broadband A range of frequencies which is sufficiently wide to accommodate one (or more) carriers modulated by digital information, typically several tens of kilohertz to several tens of megahertz.

Broadband transmission Transmission method in which a carrier is modulated by a signal prior to being passed through the transmission medium (eg, coaxial cable). Broadband transmission allows several signals to be present within a single transmission medium using *frequency division multiplexing*.

Broadband LAN A local area network which employs broadband transmission techniques.

Buffer In a *hardware* context, a buffer is a device which provides a degree of electrical isolation at an interface (the input to a buffer usually exhibits a much higher impedance than its output). In a *software* context, a buffer is a reserved area of memory which provides temporary data storage and thus may be used to compensate for a difference in the rate of data flow or time of occurrence of events.

Burst errors A form of error in which several consecutive bits within the transmitted signal are erroneous.

Bus A signal path which is invariably shared by a number of signals.

Byte A group of binary digits (*bits*) which is operated on as a unit. A byte normally comprises eight bits and thus can be used to represent a *character*.

Cable A transmission medium in which signals are passed along electrical conductors (often coaxial).

Carrier A signal (usually sinusoidal) upon which information is modulated.

Carrier sense The ability of a node to detect traffic present within a channel.

Carrier sense multiple access A protocol method which involves listening on a channel before sending. This technique allows a number of nodes to share a common transmission channel.

Channel A path between two or more points which allows data communications to take place. Channels are often derived by multiplexing and there need not be a one-to-one correspondence between *channels* and physical *circuits*.

Character A single letter, figure, punctuation symbol, or control code. Usually represented by either seven or eight bits.

Checksum A form of error checking in which the sum of all data bytes within a block is formed (any carry generated is usually discarded) and then appended to the transmitted block.

Circuit An electrical connection comprising two (a *two-wire circuit*) or four wires (a *four-wire circuit*).

Circuit switching A conventional form of switched interconnection in which a two-way circuit is provided for exclusive use during the period of connection.

Clear Act of closing a connection.

Clock A source of timing or synchronising signals.

Close Act of terminating a connection.

Coaxial cable A form of cable in which two concentric conductors are employed. The inner conductor is completely surrounded by (but electrically insulated from) the outer conductor. Coaxial cable is commonly used for both *baseband* and *broadband* LANs.

Collision A conflict within the tranmission path which is caused by two or more nodes sending information at the same time.

Collision detection The process whereby a transmitting node is able to sense a collision.

Common carrier A national organisation which provides public telecommunications services.

Concentrator A device which is used to allocate a channel to a number of users on an intelligent time division basis (see also *multiplexer*)

Congestion control A means of reducing excessive traffic in a network.

Connection A logical and/or physical relationship between the two end-points of a data link.

Contention A state which exists when two (or more) users attempt to gain control of a communication channel.

Cryptography Security protection by means of encrypted codes.

Cyclic redundancy check An error checking method in which a check character is generated by taking the remainder, after dividing all of the bits within a block of data by a predetermined binary number.

Data General term used to describe numbers, letters and symbols.

Data access arrangement Apparatus which allows data communications equipment to be connected to a common carrier network.

Data bit An individual binary digit (*bit*) which forms part of a serial bit stream in a communications system.

Database An organized collection of data present within a computer storage device. The structure of a database is usually governed by the particular application concerned.

Data link layer A layer within the ISO model for OSI which is responsible for flow control, error detection and link management.

Data set (see *modem*)

Data terminal equipment Equipment which is the ultimate source or destination of data (ie, a host computer or microcomputer or a terminal).

Deadlock State which occurs when two participating nodes are each waiting for the other to generate a message or acknowledgement and consequently no data transfer takes place.

Demodulation A process in which the original signal is recovered from a modulated carrier – the reverse of modulation. In data transmission, this process involves converting a received analog signal (ie, the modulated carrier) into a baseband digital signal.

Destination node A node within a network to which a particular message is addressed.

Dial-up method A method of communciation in which a temporary connection is established between two communicating nodes. The connection is terminated when information exchange has been successfully completed.

Dibit encoding Encoding method in which two bits are handled at a time. In *differential phase shift keying*, for example, each dibit is encoded as one of four unique carrier phase shifts (the four states for a dibit are; 00, 01, 10, and 11).

Differential modulation A modulation technique in which the coding options relate to a change in some defined parameter of the previously received signal (eg, phase angle).

Digital transmission A method of transmission which employs discrete signal levels (or *pulses*). In practice, two states known variously (and often interchangeably) as; *high/low, on/off, 1/0,* and *mark/space.*

Dumb terminal A terminal which, although it may incorporate local processing and display intelligent functions, is limited in terms of communication protocols.

Duplex Method of transmission in which information may be passed in both directions (see *full-duplex* and *half-duplex*).

Encryption A means of rendering data unreadable to unauthorized users.

Equalisation A technique used to improve the quality of a circuit by minimising distortion.

Error A condition which results when a received bit within a message is not the same state as that which was transmitted. Errors generally result from noise and distortion present in the transmission path.

Error control An arrangement, circuit or device which detects the presence of errors and which may, in some circumstances, take steps to correct the errors or request retransmission.

Error rate The probability, within a specified number of bits, characters, or blocks, of one bit being in error.

Extended binary coded decimal interchange code A code in which characters are represented as groups of eight bits and which is used primarily in IBM equipment.

File transfer protocol A protocol used to send file-structured information from one host to another.

Firmware A program (software) stored permanently in a programmable read-only memory (PROM or ROM) or semi-permanently in an erasable-programmable read-only memory (EPROM).

Flag A symbol having a special significance within a bit-oriented link protocol.

Flow control A means of controlling data transfer in order to match processing capabilities and/or the extent of buffer storage available.

Fragmentation Process of dividing a message in pieces or blocks.

Frame A unit of information at the link protocol level.

Frame check sequence The error checking informaiton for a frame (eg, a CRC).

Frequency division multiplexing Transmission technique in which a channel is shared by dividing the available bandwidth into segments occupied by different signals (ie, frequency slicing).

Frequency modulation A modulation method in which the frequency of a carrier is modified in accordance with the transmitted information.

Frequency shift keying Technique of modulating digital information onto a carrier by varying its frequency. A logic 1 bit state corresponds to one frequency while a logic 0 bit state corresponds to another frequency.

Front-end processor A dedicated processor used in conjunction with a larger computer system which handles protocol control, message handling, code conversion, error control, and other specialised functions.

Full duplex Method of transmission in which information may be passed simultaneously in both directions.

Gateway A specialised node within a network which provides a means of interconnecting networks from different vendors.

Half duplex Method of transmission in which information is passed in one direction at a time.

Handshake An interlocked sequence of signals between interconnected devices in which each device waits for an acknowledgement of its previous signal before proceeding.

Header The part of a message which contains control information.

Hierarchical network A network structure in which control is allocated at different levels according to the status of a node.

High-level data link control The link layer protocol employed in the ISO model and which employs a frame and bit structure as opposed to character protocols.

High state The more positive of the two voltage levels used to represent binary logic states. In conventional TTL logic systems, a high state (logic 1) is generally represented by a voltage in the range 2.0 V to 5.0 V.

Host computer A central computer within a data communications system which provides the primary data processing functions such as computation, database access etc.

Host-host protocol End-to-end (transport) protocol.

Inband control A transmission technique in which control information is sent over the same channel as the data.

Information bit A bit within a serial bit stream which constitutes part of the transmitted data (ie, not used for flow control or error checking).

Information frame A frame or bit sequence which contains data.

Input/output (I/O) port A circuit or functional module that allows signals to be exchanged between a microcomputer system and peripheral devices.

Interface A shared boundary between two or more systems, or between two or more elements within a system.

Interface system The functional elements required for unambiguous communications between two or more devices. Typical elements include: driver and receiver circuitry, signal line descriptions, timing and control conventions, communication protocols, and functional logic circuits.

Internet working Communication between two or more networks (which may be of different types)

Isochronous Transmission method in which all signals are of equal duration sent in a continuous sequence.

Leased line A communication line which provides a permanent connection between two nodes. Such a line is invariably leased from a telephone company.

Line driver A circuit or device which facilitates the connection of a DTE to a line and which handles any necessary level-shifting and electrical buffering in the output (*transmitted data*) path.

Line receiver A circuit or device which facilitates the connection of a line to a DTE and which handles any necessary level-shifting and electrical buffering in the input (*received data*) path.

Line turnaround The reversing of transmission direction from sender to receiver and vice versa when using a *half-duplex* circuit.

Link A channel established between two nodes within a communication system.

Listen-before-talking A system in which *carrier sense* is employed.

Listen-while-talking A system in which *collision detection* is employed.

Local area network A network which covers a limited area and which generally provides a high data rate capability. A LAN is invariably confined to a single site (ie, a building or group of buildings).

Local loop A line which links a subscriber's equipment to a local exchange.

Longitudinal redundancy check An error detection scheme in which the check character consists of bits calculated on the basis of odd or even parity on all of the characters within the block. Each bit within the longitudinal redundancy check represents a parity bit generated by considering all of the bits within the block at the same position (ie, the first bit of the LRC reflects the state of all of the first bits within the block).

Low state The more negative of the two voltage levels used to represent the binary logic states. In a conventional TTL system, a low state (logic 0) is generally represented by a voltage in the range 0 V to 0.8 V.

Memory Ability of a system to store information for later retrieval.

Message switching A term used to describe a communication system in which the participants need not be simultaneously connected together and in which data transfer takes place by message forwarding using *store and forward* techniques.

Microwave link A communication channel which employs microwave transmission.

Modem A contraction of modulator-demodulator; a device which facilitates data communication via a conventional telephone line by converting a serial data bit stream into audible signals suitable for transmission over a voice frequency telephone circuit.

Modulation Technique used for converting digital information into signals which can be passed through an analog communications channel.

Multidrop link A single line which is shared by a number of nodes. Such links often employ a master or primary node.

Multiple access A technique which relies upon nodes sensing that a channel is free before sending messages.

Multipoint link (see *multidrop link*).

Multiplexing Means by which a communications channel may be shared by several users. *Time division multiplexing* allows users to share a common channel by allocating segments of time to each. *Frequency division multiplexing* allows users to share a common channel by allocating a number of non-overlapping frequency bands (*sub-channels*) to users.

Multiplexer A device which permits *multiplexing* (see also *concentrator*).

Network A system which allows two or more computers or intelligent devices to be linked via a physical communications medium (eg, coaxial cable) in order to exchange information and share resources.

Network layer The layer within the ISO model for OSI which is responsible for services across a network.

Node An intelligent device (eg, a computer or microcomputer) present within a network. Nodes may be classified as *general-purpose* (eg, a microcomputer *host*) or may have some *network specific* function (eg, a *file server*).

Noise Any unwanted signal component which may become superimposed on a wanted signal. Various type of noise may be present; *Gaussian noise* (or *white noise*) is the random noise caused by the movement of electrons while *impulse noise* (or *black noise*) is the name given to bursts of noise (usually of very short duration) which may corrupt data.

Null modem A device (usually passive) which allows devices (each configured as a DTE) to exchange data with one another.

Octet An eight-bit data unit.

Open systems interconnection A means of interconnecting systems of different types and from different manufacturers. The ISO model for open systems interconnection comprises seven layers of protocol.

Operating system A control program which provides a low-level interface with the hardware of a microcomputer system. The operating system thus frees the programmer from the need to produce hardware specific I/O routines (eg, those associated with configuring serial I/O ports).

Optical fibre A glass or polymer fibre along which signals are propagated optically.

Out of band control A transmission technique in which control information is sent over a different channel from that occupied by the data.

Pacing A form of flow control used in systems network architecture SNA.

Packet A group of bits (comprising information and control bits arranged in a defined format) which constitutes a composite whole or *unit of information*.

Packet assembler/disassembler A device which converts asynchronous characters into packets and vice versa.

Packet switched data network A *vendor-managed* network which employs X.25 protocol to transport data between users' computers. PSDN tariffs are invariably based on the volume of data sent rather than on the distance or connect time.

Packet switching The technique used for switching within a packet switched data network in which a channel is only occupied for the duration of transmission of a packet. Packets from different users are interleaved and each is directed to its own particular destination.

Parallel transmission Method of transmission in which all of the bits which make up a character are transmitted simultaneously.

Parity bit A bit added to an asynchronously transmitted data word which is used for simple error detection (*parity checking*)

Parity check A simple error checking facility which employs a single bit. Parity may be either *even* or *odd*. The parity bit may be set to logic 1 or logic 0 to ensure that the total number of logic 1 bits present is even (*even parity*) or odd (*odd parity*). Conventionally, odd parity is used in synchronous systems while even parity is employed in asynchronous systems.

Peer entity A node which has equal status within a network (ie, a logical equal).

Peripheral An external hardware device whose activity is under the control of a computer or microcomputer system .

Phase modulation A modulation method in which the phase of a carrier is modified in accordance with the transmitted information.

Physical layer The lowest layer of the ISO model and which is concerned with the physical transmission medium, types of connector, pin connections etc.

Piggy-back A technique for data exchange in which acknowledgments are carried with messages.

Pipelining Technique by which several messages may be in passage at any one time.

Point-to-point link A network configuration in which one note is connected directly to another.

Polling Link control by a master/slave relation. The master station (eg, a computer) sends a message to each slave (eg, a terminal) in turn to ascertain whether the slave is requesting data.

Port (see *input/output port*).

Presentation layer The layer within the ISO model for OSI which resolves the differences in representation of information.

Private line (see *leased line*)

Propagation delay The time taken for a signal to travel from one point to another.

Protocol A set of rules and formats necessary for the efffective exchange of information within a data communication system.

Pulse code modulation A modulation method in which analogue signals are digitally encoded (according to approximate voltage levels) for transmission in digital form.

Qualified data A flag (X.25) which indicates how the data packet is to be interpreted.

Query A request for service.

Queue A series of messages waiting for onward transmission.

Receiver Eventual destination for the data within a data transfer.

Redundancy check A technique used for error detection in which additional bits are added such that it is possible for the receiver to detect the presence of an error in the received data.

Repeater A signal regenerator.

Residual error rate The error rate after error control processes have been applied.

Reverse channel A channel which conveys data in the opposite direction.

Ring network A network (usually a LAN) which has a circular topology.

Router A specialised node that enables communication between nodes within a LAN and an X.25 packet switched data network (also see *gateway*).

Routing The process of finding a nearly optimal path across a network. An *intermediary node* (ie, one which is neither a *source node* nor a *destination node*) is often required to have a capability which will facilitate effective routing.

Scroll mode terminal A terminal in which the data is accepted and displayed on a line-by-line basis.

Sender The source of data within a data transfer (see *transmitter*).

Serial transmission Method of transmission in which one bit is transmitted after another until all of the bits which represent a character have been sent.

Session layer The layer in the ISO model which supports the establishment, control and termination of dialogues between application processes.

Sideband The upper and lower frequency bands which contain modulated information on either side of a carrier and which are produced as a result of modulation.

Signal Information conveyed by an electrical quantity.

Signal level The relative magnitude of a signal when considered in relation to an arbitrary reference (usually expressed in volts).

Signal parameter That element of an electrical quantity whose values or sequence of values is used to convey information.

Simplex Method of transmission in which information may be passed in one direction only.

Sliding window A mechanism which indicates the frame or frames that can currently be sent.

Socket An entry and/or exit point (also see *I/O port*).

Source node A node within a network which is the originator of a particular message.

Source routing A process which determines the path or route of data at the source of the message.

Start bit The first bit (normally a *space*) of an asynchronously transmitted data word which alerts the receiving equipment to the arrival of a character.

Start/stop signalling Asynchronous transmission of characters.

Statistical multiplexer (see *concentrator*).

Stop and wait protocol A protocol which involves waiting for an acknowledgment (eg, ACK) before sending another message.

Stop bits The last bit (or bits), normally *mark*, of an asynchronously transmitted data word which signals that the line is about to be placed in its *rest state*.

Store and forward A process in which a message or *packet* is stored temporarily before onward transmission.

Supervisory frame A control frame.

Switching A means of conveying information from source to destination across a network.

Synchronization Establishing known timing relationships.

Synchronous data link control IBM standard communication protocol which replaces *binary synchronous communications*.

Synchronous transmission Method of transmission in which data is transmitted at a fixed rate and in which the transmitter and receiver are both synchronised.

Tandem A network configuration in which two or more point-to-point circuits are linked together with transmission effected on an end-to-end basis over all links.

Terminal server A special-purpose node which allows a number of terminals to be connected to a network via a single physical line. A terminal server thus frees network nodes from the burden of establishing connections between local terminals and remote nodes. Terminals connected to a terminal server will, of course, have access to all nodes present within the network.

Time division multiplexing Transmission technique in which users share a common channel by allocating segments of time to each (ie, time slicing).

Time sharing A method of operation in which a computer facility is shared by a number of users. The computer divides its processing time between the users and a high speed of processing ensures that each user is unaware of the demands of others and processing appears to be virtually instantaneous.

Timeout Period during which a pre-determined time interval has to elapse before further action is taken (usually as a result of no response from another node).

Token A recognizable control mechanism used to control access to a network.

Topology The structure of a network and which is usually described in the form of a diagram which shows the nodes and links between them.

Traffic analysis Process of determining the flow and volume of traffic within a network.

Transceiver A transmitter/receiver.

Transmitter Source of data (see *sender*).

Transparency A property of a network that allows users to access and transfer information without being aware of the physical, electrical and logical characteristics of the network.

Transport layer The layer of the ISO model for OSI which describes host-host communication.

Tribit encoding Encoding method in which three bits are handled at a time.

Un-numbered frame A control frame.

V-series A series of recommendations specified by the CCITT which defines analog interface and modem standards for data communications over common carrier lines such as a PSDN.

Vertical redundancy check An error detection scheme in which one bit of each data word (the *parity bit*) is set to logic 1 or logic 0 so that the total number of logic 1 bits is odd (*odd parity*) or even (*even parity*).

Virtual circuit An arrangement which provides a sequenced, error-free delivery of data.

Voice-grade line A conventional telephone connection.

Wide area network A network which covers a relatively large geographical area (eg, one which spans a large region, country or continent).

Wideband A communications channel which exhibits a very much greater bandwidth than that associated with a conventional voice-grade channel and which will support data rates of typically between 10k and 500 kbps.

Work station A general-purpose node within a network which provides users with processing power, and which thus invariably includes a microcomputer.

X-series A series of recommendations specified by the CCITT which defines digital data communications over common carrier lines such as a PSDN.

Zero insertion Transparency method for bit-orientated link protocols.

Index

Semiconductor devices